PRAISE FOR *DIRTY GOD*

"Johnnie Moore is this generation's Billy Graham. He has quickly become one of the nation's most powerful voices on understanding and connecting with God—especially for this generation. Moore's words strip away dusty, stale preconceptions and introduce us to a very real Savior who pursues us through the grit and grime of life and who would do anything to let you know how much He loves you."

—KAREN KINGSBURY
#1 *NEW YORK TIMES* BEST-SELLING NOVELIST
AUTHOR OF *THE BRIDGE* AND *THE CHANCE*

"Jesus gives us grace to us and through us. This brings glory to God, good to others, and gladness to us. This book invites us to both get and give God's grace."

—MARK DRISCOLL
FOUNDING PASTOR, MARS HILL CHURCH
CO-FOUNDER, ACTS 29 CHURCH PLANTING NETWORK
FOUNDER, RESURGENCE
#1 *NEW YORK TIMES* BEST-SELLING AUTHOR

"A lifetime of coaching couples to relational health has convinced me of at least one thing: grace, understood and lived, changes lives. Johnnie writes about a profound subject in a deeply empathic and practical way. He writes like you're chatting over coffee about something you've been searching for your whole life."

—GARY SMALLEY
AUTHOR OF *THE DNA OF RELATIONSHIPS*

"From people that are far from God to the people that walk with him daily, we are all undeserving of God's grace. In his book, *Dirty God*, Johnnie Moore provides an honest perspective on God's unorthodox approach to save the world he created. New believers and seasoned Christians alike will appreciate this book's challenge to receive and share the grace of God without limits."

—STEVEN FURTICK
LEAD PASTOR, ELEVATION CHURCH
AUTHOR OF *GREATER*

"Too many people see God as a safe, antiseptic, distant Being. They find him nice enough, far off as he is, during their lives, but are scared of him when they face death. In this book, Johnnie Moore confronts us with a God who, in Jesus Christ, joins us in the mud and blood and dust of our lives. This book will make you reconsider the way you think, the way you pray, and the way you talk to your neighbors."

—RUSSELL D. MOORE
DEAN, SOUTHERN BAPTIST THEOLOGICAL SEMINARY

"Jesus wasn't content to simply observe the ill-fated future of the world. He climbed down into it, and sacrificed life and limb to make it a better place. Johnnie is leading a generation back into the trenches with Jesus. They will not be content to leave the world as broken as they found it. This book is their manifesto."

—CHRISTINE CAINE
DIRECTOR OF EQUIP AND EMPOWER MINISTRIES
FOUNDER OF THE A21 CAMPAIGN

"Johnnie Moore is one of Christianity's most promising next-generation leaders."

—JOHNNY HUNT
PASTOR, FIRST BAPTIST CHURCH OF WOODSTOCK, GEORGIA
FORMER PRESIDENT, SOUTHERN BAPTIST CONVENTION

"Grace explained is helpful but grace experienced changes everything. Johnny Moore in his book *Dirty God* does more than explain grace but through his powerful and personal examples he helps us experience grace."

—KYLE IDLEMAN
TEACHING PASTOR, SOUTHEAST CHRISTIAN CHURCH
AUTHOR OF *NOT A FAN*

"It's rare to find a leader who communicates as clearly and with as much humility and transparency as Johnnie Moore. Not only will his new book, *Dirty God*, show you how to get grace—it will inspire you to give grace to a world that is in great need."

—JENTEZEN FRANKLIN
SENIOR PASTOR, FREE CHAPEL
NEW YORK TIMES BEST-SELLING AUTHOR OF *FASTING*

"Think you understand grace? Think again. Johnnie's book delivers revelation after revelation on a subject that is essential to us all."

—ANDY ANDREWS
NEW YORK TIMES BEST-SELLING AUTHOR OF *HOW DO YOU KILL 11
MILLION PEOPLE?*, *THE NOTICER*, AND *THE TRAVELER'S GIFT*

"Every earthly exposition on God's grace will always fall short in unveiling its eternal efficacy . . . but this book comes incredibly close. Like a pair of misplaced glasses that have been found, *Dirty God* brings God's grace into focus in a way that will shatter our misconceptions and shape our future."

—PASTOR BOB COY
CALVARY CHAPEL, FORT LAUDERDALE

"I appreciate Johnnie Moore's heart for the things of God and his desire to see believers live their lives as agents of His grace. *Dirty God* is essential reading for anyone interested in gaining a deeper grasp of the free, life-transforming power of grace."

—JIM DALY
PRESIDENT, FOCUS ON THE FAMILY

"*Dirty God* is a must-read for anyone who desires to become a person of grace, not just for yourself, but to make a maximum impact on the hurting world around you. Johnnie is such an incredible communicator and writes on a message that I believe our world needs more than ever."

—PETE WILSON
SENIOR PASTOR, CROSS POINT CHURCH

"Grace is the underpinning of everything God offers us. With a deeply personal narrative approach, Johnnie draws you into the heart of God's grace and challenges you to both experience it and guide others to it."

—DR. JOHN TOWNSEND
LEADERSHIP CONSULTANT AND BEST-
SELLING AUTHOR OF *BOUNDARIES*

"There are few young leaders out there who can speak with the clarity and direction of Johnnie Moore. Johnnie will challenge you."

—DR. TIM CLINTON
PRESIDENT, AMERICAN ASSOCIATION OF CHRISTIAN COUNSELORS

"I love the way Johnnie Moore writes. In *Dirty God*, he captures the call to share grace in a way that is raw and honest and hopeful. We need more books like this."

—JON ACUFF
WALL STREET JOURNAL BEST-SELLING AUTHOR OF
QUITTER AND *STUFF CHRISTIANS LIKE*

"This book is an amazing reminder of the power of God's grace. All fall short of the glory of God, but the sacrifice of the cross is an unending source of redemption to all who seek it. The grace of the Lord is so revolutionary in that He often uses flawed people to achieve great things. Johnnie Moore writes in such a profound yet simple style, in a way that is sure to connect with the reader no matter where they are in their walk with God. *Dirty God* has such a powerful message about God's grace, one that is quite often overlooked."

—PASTOR MATTHEW BARNETT
CO-FOUNDER OF THE DREAM CENTER

"There is nothing more difficult for us to get our minds around than the grace of God. Even those of us who have tasted the radical saving grace of God find it intuitively difficult not to put conditions on grace. 'Don't take it too far; keep it balanced,' we say. The truth is, though, that the biggest lie Satan wants the church to believe is that grace is dangerous and therefore needs to be kept in check: 'Yes grace but' originated with the devil in Genesis 3. My friend Johnnie Moore has written a book on grace that needs to be read and wrestled with. Johnnie believes that the gospel of grace is *way* more drastic, *way* more offensive, *way* more liberating, *way* more shocking, and *way* more counterintuitive than any of us realize. So do I. Read this book."

—TULLIAN TCHIVIDJIAN
PASTOR OF CORAL RIDGE PRESBYTERIAN CHURCH
AUTHOR OF *JESUS + NOTHING = EVERYTHING*

"*Dirty God* is a well-written and grace-saturated treatment of the Christian life. The author, Johnnie Moore, is convinced that God's grace changes everything. It changes us and it changes the world around us. Just as God was willing to get his hands dirty in demonstrating his love for us, so we can get our hands dirty in being a conduit of God's grace for others."

—DR. BRUCE ASHFORD
DEAN OF THE COLLEGE, SOUTHEASTERN
BAPTIST THEOLOGICAL SEMINARY

"Johnnie Moore takes you on an amazing journey around the world, through space and time, to bring you back to the personal revelation of God's grace for you."

—JAMES ROBISON
FOUNDER/PRESIDENT, LIFE OUTREACH INTERNATIONAL

"The heart of the gospel of grace is a Savior who did not consider equality with God something to be grasped, but assumed the role of a slave to save His creation. Moore exposes the truth of God's Word, and the glory of the incarnation. He is the God who is near, God with us."

—ED STETZER
PRESIDENT, LIFEWAY RESEARCH

"The world needs more grace. Grace flows from the heart of Jesus to people. And people with grace-infused, grace-transformed, grace-empowered lives become the sacred glue that puts our broken world back together. In *Dirty God*, Johnnie will bring you face-to-face with grace. And you'll be transformed to become a transformer in this world."

—DERWIN L. GRAY
LEAD PASTOR, TRANSFORMATION CHURCH
WWW.TRANSFORMATIONCHURCH.TC
@DERWINLGRAY

"*Dirty God* is a tremendous resource that will help you understand God's amazing grace in deeper and powerful ways and equip you to share it with others. Johnnie pulls no punches as he shows how God meets us in the mess of our lives and I, for one, am so thankful."

—JUD WILHITE
SENIOR PASTOR, CENTRAL CHRISTIAN CHURCH
AUTHOR OF *TORN*

"This book is one of a kind. It takes on both Christianity and "Christianity" head-on with no holds barred and mercilessly separates the sheep from the goats. If "Christians" are putting you off Christ, read this book. In fact, no matter who you are or what you believe, read this book. It's good for those who know Christ and better still for those who don't."

—DOUGLAS GRESHAM
STEPSON OF C. S. LEWIS
EXECUTIVE PRODUCER, *THE CHRONICLES OF NARNIA*

"It's rare for an author to be able to write well about something old, but *Dirty God* has remarkably given us 'grace' anew. This book is fresh, and filled with fascinating stories. It is theological, but entirely approachable. This is one you can't put down, and it will change you, it really will."

—MILES MCPHERSON
SENIOR PASTOR, THE ROCK CHURCH

"Christians must recognize their dependency on the undeserved, freely given grace of God, not only for salvation but for meeting the challenges of life. Johnnie Moore challenges our tendency to be presumptuous recipients of God's grace. *Dirty God* reminds us of the cost to God in granting us love and mercy. Through this convicting and articulate duo of stories and biblical truth, you will be stirred to be a channel of God's grace to a lost and hurting world."

—JERRY RANKIN
PRESIDENT EMERITUS, INTERNATIONAL MISSION BOARD, SBC

"As a champion for children in poverty for over thirty years, I encourage you to read this book. Johnnie reminds us that grace is both the most accessible and powerful gift a person has at their disposal. The vision of grace described in *Dirty God* has the potential to change the world."

—DR. WESS STAFFORD
PRESIDENT /CEO, COMPASSION INTERNATIONAL

"I love Johnnie Moore's new book, *Dirty God*. Johnnie does us a favor by bringing us back to basics: the Cross of Christ changed everything! God got down in the trenches with us and extends grace to the least, the last, and the lost. This book will lead you to a deeper understanding of grace in your own life, and God will use it to make you salt and light to a world so desperate for authentic Christianity."

—BOB CRESON
PRESIDENT/CEO, WYCLIFFE BIBLE TRANSLATORS USA

"Any authentic teaching about grace should both lift us up to God and send us out to others. This accessible, lively, and well-written book does both!"

—REVEREND CANON J. JOHN
SPEAKER AND AUTHOR

"Johnnie Moore writes with a refreshing passion."

—LUIS PALAU
WORLD EVANGELIST

"Johnnie Moore is one of the most dynamic leaders of his generation. The fascinating perspective he provides in *Dirty God* is one that will both challenge and empower every Christ Follower who reads it. We serve a God who wasn't afraid to reach out to us, wherever we are, no matter how far we've fallen. Johnnie's words are full of power, conviction, and grace . . . a message of hope that so many are longing to hear."

—VERNON BREWER
FOUNDER AND PRESIDENT, WORLD HELP

"*Dirty God* is a must-read on grace. Johnnie Moore goes far beyond the everyday messages on grace and exposes us to the side of God that's a bit dirty, and requires you to get dirty too. Moore's message strikes a nerve deep in the soul when he explains how grace means you must do something! You must act. You must get your hands dirty, like Jesus did for you. And when you live like this, the grace of God begins to heal others—through your grace and love."

—PALMER CHINCHEN, PhD
AUTHOR OF *TRUE RELIGION: TAKING PIECES OF HEAVEN TO PLACES OF HELL ON EARTH* AND *GOD CAN'T SLEEP*

"I don't know a better communicator than Johnnie Moore. His speaking and writing is practical, interesting, and truly transformational. *Dirty God* is his best work yet. Truly an amazing book."

—CLAYTON KING
PRESIDENT, CROSSROADS MINISTRIES
AUTHOR AND TEACHING PASTOR, NEWSPRING CHURCH

"In *Dirty God*, Johnnie Moore powerfully weaves compelling theological truth with rich imagery and captivating stories to move his readers to a deeper understanding of the profound implications of God's grace. He somehow does this in a way that is inviting to the skeptic, yet challenging to the believer; which leads me to heartily recommend this book!"

—WERNER CLOETE
SOUTH AFRICAN TEACHER
AUTHOR OF *FIRST CLASS: THE CALLING AND IMPACT OF A CHRISTIAN TEACHER*

"Rarely has someone been able to write on such a profound topic in such an accessible way. Johnnie is a master storyteller, and in *Dirty God* he strikes the chord of grace for a new generation. This book is one of those books that people will talk about for a long time."

—Josh McDowell,
Author of *More Than a Carpenter*

DIRTY GOD

JOHNNIE MOORE

THOMAS NELSON
Since 1798

NASHVILLE   DALLAS   MEXICO CITY   RIO DE JANEIRO

Published in Nashville, Tennessee, by Thomas Nelson. Thomas Nelson is a registered trademark of Thomas Nelson, Inc.

Thomas Nelson, Inc., titles may be purchased in bulk for educational, business, fund-raising, or sales promotional use. For information, please e-mail SpecialMarkets@ThomasNelson.com.

Unless otherwise noted, Scripture quotations are taken from the Holy Bible, New International Version®, NIV®. Copyright © 1973, 1978, 1984, 2011 by Biblica, Inc.™ Used by permission of Zondervan. All rights reserved worldwide. www.zondervan.com. All quotations are from the 2011 edition unless otherwise noted.

Scripture quotations marked GNT are from THE GOOD NEWS TRANSLATION. © 1976, 1992 by The American Bible Society. Used by permission. All rights reserved.

Scripture quotations marked KJV are from the King James Version (public domain).

Scripture quotations marked MSG are from The Message by Eugene H. Peterson. © 1993, 1994, 1995, 1996, 2000. Used by permission of NavPress Publishing Group. All rights reserved.

Scripture quotations marked NKJV are from THE NEW KING JAMES VERSION. © 1982 by Thomas Nelson, Inc. Used by permission. All rights reserved.

Library of Congress Cataloging-in-Publication Data Available Upon Request

978-0-8499-6451-0

Printed in the United States of America

12 13 14 15 16 QG 6 5 4 3 2 1

My dear Andrea, this book, too, is dedicated to you.
It's been written from the deepest part of my heart,
a place only you know.
So somehow we must have written it together.
You must be the most loved girl in the entire world.

CONTENTS

CONTENTS

FOREWORD

GOD KNOWS EVERYTHING ABOUT YOU. HE knows every thought you've had, every step you've taken, every word you've spoken. He knows every sin, stumble, and foolish mistake you've ever made. He knows all things you've seen and done that make you want to run and hide. And yet, God loves you.

Johnnie is a leader who deeply understands the depths of God's love and lives in a graceful lifestyle of love to others. Johnnie writes an important message to the next generation about something our culture can't fully understand: the grace of God. This grace can't be earned, bought, or sold. Grace is a gift of God through Jesus Christ. Too few people actually know who Jesus is, that he came to earth to live the perfect life you couldn't and to die the death you deserved because he loves you and wants to spend eternity with you.

In the book of Romans, Paul urges us to fully surrender our lives to God in worship as a response to God's grace: "So then, my friends, because of God's great mercy to us . . . offer yourselves as a living sacrifice to God, dedicated to his service and pleasing to him. This is the true worship that you should offer" (Rom. 12:1 TEV). Grace changes us and makes us respond in gratitude to a God who changes us from the inside out. You cannot change on your own. If you could, you would—but you can't, so you won't. It's by Jesus' power that our lives are changed.

God doesn't expect you to be perfect, but he does insist on complete honesty. The sooner we give up the illusion that the Church must be perfect in order to love it, the sooner we quit pretending and start admitting we're all imperfect and need grace. This is the beginning of real community. Every church could put out a sign "No perfect people need apply. This is a place only for those who admit they are sinners, need grace, and want to grow."

I join with Johnnie's call for everyone who has received God's grace to bring this message to every nation: because of God's grace, Jesus is a "friend of sinners." There is nothing you can do to make Jesus stop loving you. He chooses to reach into the mess and dirtiness of our lives to give us a past forgiven, a purpose for living, and a home in heaven.

RICK WARREN
AUTHOR OF THE PURPOSE DRIVEN LIFE
SENIOR PASTOR, SADDLEBACK CHURCH

INTRODUCTION

MANY YEARS AGO, A GROUP OF INTELLECTU-
als, academics, theologians, and philosophers sat in the Senior
Common Room at Magdalen College, Oxford, deep in discussion of what particular quality, unique to Christianity, makes it
superior to, or at least different from, the many great religions of
mankind.

One of the group, looking up through the fog of tobacco
smoke, saw the young fellow of English, C. S. Lewis, walk into
the Common Room with his brother, the historian W. H. Lewis.
"Well, there's Jack Lewis—he's a Christian. Let's ask him," he said.

All nodded, knowing that at the very least, Jack would add
something of interest to the conversation.

"I say, Jack," called one of them across the room. "What is it
that makes Christianity stand out above all the other great religions of the world?"

Without even a split second of hesitation, Jack replied in his
powerful voice, "That's easy—it's grace."

There was a moment of thoughtful silence, followed by a
round of gentle, understated applause from the few Christians
present.[1]

———

This is a book about grace.

And how grace split time in half and made a broken world a playground again for the goodness and kindness of God.

PART 1

GETTING GRACE

ONE

—

CHISHTI'S ROSES

AJMER ISN'T A PLACE OF GREAT SIGNIFICANCE to most people. It's an almost invisible town—a small outpost of life crunched into the lifeless deserts of western India along the Pakistan border. Ajmer is a place where a gaggle of everyday Indians live their common lives unnoticed by the greater world. They drink their chai, raise their families, work hard, and then die. The pages of history flip with nary an incident in Ajmer, where people:

Wake up.

Have tea.

Work.

Eat.

Work.

Go home.

Sleep.

Wake up . . .

That's Ajmer—a sleepy little Indian village.

Unless you're a devotee of the major mystical sect of Islam in India, Sufism, then insignificant Ajmer is to you the most important place on planet Earth. It is your particular Mecca, and you

3

live and will die revering it. On all the planet, there isn't a place for which your faith has more affection.

This is what brought *me* to Ajmer.

A JOURNEY TO BELIEVE

I arrived in Ajmer in the middle of my own personal pilgrimage of India's major religions. I was "kicking their tires" to see what might seem legitimate, and I was trying desperately to understand why their devotees believed what they believed about Hinduism, Buddhism, Jainism, Islam, and Sikhism.

Ajmer was the next stop on a journey that had already taken me to other obscure places, such as Pushkar, one of the oldest cities in India, which hugs a tiny pond in which adherents ceremonially bathe each morning. Pushkar is most famous for its annual camel caravan and, most important, for one of India's only temples to the Hindu creator, Brahma. Before Pushkar, I had visited the important Islamic cities of Jaipur and Agra; the holiest Hindu city, Varanasi; the city of the Sikhs, Amritsar; and the mountaintop village of the Dalai Lama, McLeod Ganj.

I must have smelled of the divine by the time my train arrived in the city of the Sufis. I also smelled of some other, less appetizing flavors of travel.

The potent religious significance of Ajmer resides in a single shrine that draws millions of devotees from around the world. It sits unobtrusively at the foot of the Taragarh hill, surrounded by a group of ramshackle marble buildings. Only in India do the terms *ramshackle* and *marble* work in the same sentence. And only in India would such an important place be crammed into a corner at the foot of a hill. India is, above all, dripping in the sacred.

Each building in the complex was donated by one of India's great Muslim emperors, over hundreds of years of veneration.

You arrive through a massive and ornate gate given by a maharaja from southern India. There is also a mosque named after the Muslim Mughal emperor Akbar the Great, donated by his grandson Shah Jahan (who also constructed the Taj Mahal).

And then there's the shrine where the entombed body of Moinuddin Chishti has lain since the early thirteenth century. This shrine gleams in the harsh Indian sun. Its magnetism has attracted myriad worshippers from every stratum of society, from nations around the world, for hundreds of years.

Akbar the Great, who had anything he wanted in the entire world at his beck and call, would nevertheless embark each year on a four-hundred-kilometer journey by foot to visit the shrine, erecting large pillars memorializing his journey every few kilometers along the way.

Chishti's shrine was hypnotizing to the powerful Akbar, and its enchantment seemed just as palpable on the day of my own journey there, as I watched thousands of people come to pay homage.

SMELLING ROSES

The circular shrine isn't very large. Devotees slip through a tiny entrance and worship by circling clockwise around the gold-plated casket of Chishti. Hours of travel, thousands of dollars, and tons of frustration culminate in a passing glance at the casket of a centuries-gone Sufi saint.

Actually, it's a little more like pushing than walking. The circle could comfortably hold a couple of dozen people, but typically hundreds cram into the shrine, all elbowing each other and complaining as they move at a snail's pace around the casket, creeping centimeter by centimeter.

What I most remember about the inside of the shrine was the nearly intoxicating smell.

Devotees of Chishti customarily bring with them red rose petals as an offering to the entombed saint. They carry the large baskets over their heads as they navigate around the coffin, say a brief prayer, and then dump the rose petals over the shrine. The lack of ventilation causes the smell of the roses to hover like trapped smoke in the tiny room. It's inebriating.

By the time I made it out the sliver of a door, I was already light-headed. The mystical aroma of Chishti's roses clung to my clothing, leaving its sweet smell lingering in my wake for hours.

People must have been able to tell I had visited Chishti's tomb. I was one of thousands walking through dusty alleyways accompanied by the curious scent of a rose.

Then there were the "demon-possessed" man and the elderly lady worshipping frantically outside the shrine.

The man was lying on the marble floor, shaking violently and foaming at the mouth. The young Sufi leader showing us around told me that he was "possessed by spirits" and that his family had traveled a long way to lay him outside of the shrine in the hope that

Chishti would be gracious enough to cleanse him of the evil that was controlling him. The saint was their last-ditch effort to free their loved one of the terror plaguing him.

They had traveled for days, desperate for help. They had thrown hundreds of rose petals on his casket and sat outside his shrine for hours, begging and pleading.

They had probably participated in the common practice of tying strings to the gate that clung to the external wall of the shrine. Each string represented a particular prayer request, and it would remain there until Chishti answered their request. Then they would remove the string from the saint's divine to-do list.

There were hundreds, maybe thousands, of strings tied to the gate. Some had been there so long that the elements had rotted them.

Chishti must have been preoccupied.

In the shadow of the string gate lay the elderly woman whose face remains branded onto my own story. Her wrinkles testified to a long and difficult life, and this day was clearly one of her most difficult.

She lay on her side, her aged fingers clinging to the gate where the strings were tied. In fact, she seemed to be holding on to a string I assumed was her own, her knuckles white with desperation as she prayed intensely for the saint's attention.

Her words were thumping like hammers on the exterior of Chishti's shrine. She was pleading her case.

I wish I knew exactly what she was praying for. Maybe a grandchild or a friend was sick, or maybe a loved one was enduring some impossible financial situation. Maybe she was asking God for the strength to live on after the death of her husband, or maybe the desert sun had lapped up the rain on her family farm and drought was draining them of food and a future.

I have no idea what was consuming that dear woman's heart that day, but one thing was blatantly clear—she was desperate.

She wasn't praying one of those halfhearted, before-you-gobble-down-a-Thanksgiving-turkey types of prayers. She was praying the kind of prayer someone prays when it's a matter of life or death, when things look hopeless—when a miracle seems to be the only possible solution. The kind you pray when you feel as if you're in a tomb yourself, hopelessly crushed by life's troubles, and the only solution is a resurrection. Resurrections are miracles, and miracles seem sadly hard to come by when you need them the most.

She was begging Chishti for a dose of grace.

Meanwhile, Chishti lay there in his own tomb, surrounded by the incandescent scent of roses. Dead.

Maybe, by now, her string has rotted off that gate.

DESPERATE FOR GOD

This desperation to get to God gnaws at us, doesn't it? It's like a hunger pang that quietly signals to us that we need some nutrients.

This hunger has fueled man's ancient pursuit of God in its great variety of incarnations around the world, through all the world's religious systems. For sure, it was this hunger that pushed me to India, and this hunger that is causing me to type these words, and it's probably this hunger that causes you to read them too.

We are more than curious about God. We are compelled to find out what kind of God he is, and whether he cares at all about us. And even when we're most tempted to run away from him, we always find that, like Jonah, we fail to do so.

I've spent much of my young life wandering around the world trying to satiate this hunger myself, and the more I try to feed it, or to run away from it, somehow it's still there. It knocks on my heart. God seems so elusive—and yet he's somehow always there.

All the religions of the world are after God's attention. They throw their roses, tie their strings, and plead for their deity to give them—at least—a passing glance.

Muslims have their "Five Pillars." Sikhs have their "Five K's." Hindus ring bells when they enter their temples to awaken their gods to their presence. Muslims pray fives times a day and steady their lives on the Koran, and every day Hindu priests on the banks of the Ganges River scream, plead, bang metal, twirl fire, and ring bells to try to attract the attention of any one of their many gods.

All of that racket and ruckus, all of that noise and devotion, is informed by one simple belief: men and women believe they have to work very hard to get their gods to turn their faces toward them.

It's the same all through history: man begging his God for grace, and doing everything he can to earn it.

A cacophony of worship has risen wildly into the sky for centuries as people grasp frantically for the attention of a god. Some god. Their god.

But Jesus changed things. He told a different story. He taught, and millions of Christians through the ages have discovered, a different kind of God. Jesus' teaching gave birth to the only religious system in the world that breaks through the racket of worship with a simple message: the real God is a God who delights in giving grace.

We can stop trying so hard to get his attention.

We already have it.

TWO

—

TALKING SMACK
TO FAKE GODS

GRACE ACCEPTS US AS WE ARE.

Because of this, God's story, through history, is filled with people whom we would probably have passed over.

Take Elijah, for instance. He was one of God's prophets in the Old Testament. God chose him to speak on his behalf to his people at a particularly unflattering moment of their own story. They had become fascinated with a kind of pagan worship that involved unimaginable rituals. They had long forgotten the God who had freed them from Egyptian bondage.

At that unpleasant time, God sent Elijah as his spokesperson to his wandering people.

You would expect Elijah to have it all together—to be the kind of guy who had never had a bad day, who had never yelled at his mom. To be the goody-two-shoes type who never smoked a cigarette or said a bad word. To be the type of person who doesn't lose his temper and has never considered suicide.

In short, you would expect him to be prime prophet material, right?

When you actually read the story of Elijah, you find a story that's altogether different. Elijah was a basket case! His emotions were up one minute, down the next, and his greatest achievement was followed by a colossal failure. He was sometimes doubtful and even angry with God.

Not to mention, Elijah became so depressed at one point that he nearly killed himself! His relationship with God "depended on the day."

And you know what?

Elijah wasn't the exception.

God's Old Testament prophets had their fair share of drama. Jonah was swallowed by a fish because of blatant disobedience, David had an affair, Jeremiah was a crybaby, Isaiah once walked naked and barefoot for three *years* to make a point, Ezekiel lay on his side for over a year as an illustration of God's relationship with his people, and Hosea married a prostitute.

And don't forget our buddy Elisha's crowning moment: "As he was walking along the road, some boys came out of the town and jeered at him. 'Get out of here, baldy!' they said. 'Get out of here, baldy!'" (2 Kings 2:23).

How did Elisha respond?

He didn't exactly turn the other cheek. Instead: "He turned around, looked at them, and called down a curse on them in the name of the LORD" (v. 24).

One thing is sure: the great heroes of biblical history had plenty of issues. If they were living today, they would headline tabloids and star in reality shows.

God has a track record of giving grace to rookie leaders— an approach that seems absurd when you consider that most of the great figures I've encountered in the other religions of the world have become famous by their *perfection*. The very reason that they are priests or prophets, saints or monks, is because they lived nearly flawless lives of pure devotion.

Yet Jesus taught us that his Father was the kind of God who picked regular people and then used them in powerful ways despite their imperfections.

In fact, nearly all of the great stories of the Bible are stories of God using an imperfect person. In the end, it is God who is the star of the show—and Elijah's most famous triumph was no exception.

Actually, the whole thing was worth watching on pay-per-view.

WHEN GOD SHOWED UP

As a child, I had an unfortunate obsession with professional wrestling. My dad and I watched each week as grown men, in carefully choreographed routines, pummeled each other to death. They created and fueled rivalries, jumped off poles, punched and kicked, twisted and tortured, and eventually pinned their opponents. Even more unfortunately, all of this was done by men wearing what was basically a Speedo!

Eventually these rivalries became so intense that there had to be one final, conclusive contest. For weeks ahead of time, the promoters would air commercials and put up posters and billboards, and fans would shell out millions on pay-per-view television to see the final showdown between archenemies in a deadly "cage match."

This would be the decisive battle; the winner would be declared champion.

The combatants would be locked into an arena, and the door *chained shut*! The audience would watch in fevered anticipation, and one thing was guaranteed—there would be a winner and a loser. One guy would come out bloodied but victorious, and the other would be incapacitated, lying there in shame and defeat. The cage match would spell the end of the rivalry.

Elijah's ancient showdown with the prophets of Baal was a cage match.

There would be no ambiguity. They would fight until the end. Except that in Elijah's case, there was no choreography, the stakes were higher, and this moment would be *the* moment when the ancient war between the pagan god Baal and Jehovah would be settled once and for all.

In 1 Kings, we learn that it was the confident Elijah who challenged the prophets of Baal to this showdown. The rules were simple: whichever God sent fire from heaven to consume a readied sacrifice would be declared *the one true God*.

The prophets of Baal were the first to try. They spent all day yelling their mantras to Baal. They even started cutting themselves to demonstrate to their god how serious they were about all of this. They danced and pleaded and bled—from morning till evening.

Remember—Elijah was a bit rough around the edges. There's a sarcastic edge to him in the biblical account. As the prophets of Baal became louder and louder, and as their praying went longer and longer, Elijah began to taunt them.

In 1 Kings 18:27, he barked at them, "Shout louder! . . . Surely he is a god! Perhaps he is deep in thought, or busy, or traveling. Maybe he is sleeping and must be awakened." Elijah's Hebrew word for *busy* is sometimes translated to imply that Baal might be indisposed. (For the less sophisticated among us, *indisposed* is a word that polite people use to refer to someone who is sitting on the toilet.)

I like Elijah.

He's feisty.

He's gritty.

He's human.

I think God liked him too.

Elijah wasn't just going to sit on the sidelines, watching these pagan priests fail at jarring their god from his lethargy. Elijah threw insults at them. He was like a football player from Georgia or Texas. He wasn't content just to know that he was going to win, and that his team was the strongest, fastest, and best. No, he wanted glory in his victory. He wanted to make sure the other team knew that they were weaker, slower, second-rate. Elijah was the kind of guy who puffed out his chest, chewed a little tobacco sometimes, and rubbed in a victory.

And after a whole day of exasperated babbling by the prophets of Baal, when there was blood and chaos everywhere, it was finally Elijah's turn.

Elijah might have had his ups and downs, but when he had faith, he had Teflon faith. He knew beyond a doubt that there was something drastically different about Jehovah, the God of Israel—the one true God.

So Elijah did something risky. He turned things up a notch.

He asked that the altar to Jehovah be saturated with water—once, twice, three times. Not only would God have to send fire from heaven to consume that sacrifice, he would have to do it with soaking-wet wood and a soaking-wet sacrifice.

The biography of Elijah records this iconic moment:

At the time of sacrifice, the prophet Elijah stepped forward and prayed: "Lord, the God of Abraham, Isaac and Israel, let it be known today that you are God in Israel and that I am your servant and have done all these things at your command. Answer me, Lord, answer me, so these people will know that you, Lord, are God, and that you are turning their hearts back again." (1 Kings 18:36–37)

The response was instantaneous: "Then the fire of the Lord fell and burned up the sacrifice, the wood, the stones and the soil, and also licked up the water in the trench" (v. 38).

The people who had been watching the whole affair were flabbergasted. The author said that they immediately fell flat on their faces and cried out, "The Lord—he is God!" (v. 39).

This was a formidable, spine-tingling moment.

Maybe you've read this story a half dozen times. Maybe it has become a little stale. It shouldn't be. This moment demands the full engagement of your imagination. It is epic.

Think of the moment in the movie *Gladiator* when Maximus reveals his identity to the illegitimate emperor. Think of the scene in *Braveheart* when William Wallace declares, "They may take our lives, but they will never take our freedom!" When you watch those scenes, excitement runs up your spine and works its way out through goose bumps on your skin. Multiply that a hundred-fold, and that's the feeling you should associate with the moment God sent fire to consume the altar in full view of the desperate, disappointed, humbled, bloodied, hoarse, and enraged prophets of Baal.

Hundreds of people had been watching this death match play out all day long—and then suddenly, spontaneously, all of those spectators fell on their faces, loudly declaring their worship and support of Elijah's God—the victor! If you had witnessed it, you, too, would have fallen flat on your face in awe and worship.

What was most stunning to the people was that Elijah's God didn't require a theatrical performance to spur him to action. Elijah didn't have to make a big scene, scream till his voice was raw, or mar his flesh. It was as if Jehovah had been sitting on the edge of heaven, with his feet hanging off the ledge, waiting for the moment he was asked to intervene. He was *eager* to respond to the request of his servant. He wanted to help, and he didn't have to be asked twice.

He had a whole bucket of undeserved kindness, called *grace*, to pour all over those idolatrous children he loved so much.

This God, Jehovah, was unique. He was different from Baal, and he's different from every other idea of God. It's his grace that makes him unique.

It seemed as if he *wanted* to be in the lives of his people, and he didn't wait until their worship was loud or their repentance was sufficiently humiliating. He didn't wait until they bugged him enough that, desperate, he responded just to get them to stop.

This God was waiting by the phone. He was listening for it to ring. He was ready when his people needed him to care.

And in the most critical moment, he responded.

But why?

Why did he jump at the request of his servant Elijah? Why did he allow himself to be pulled into this magic show? Isn't throwing down fire from heaven a little below him?

And why didn't he just write off these people who'd long forgotten him?

The key is in this phrase: "Answer me, LORD, answer me, so these people will know that you, LORD, are God, and that you are turning their hearts back again" (v. 37).

This is a God who *cares* about his people and who *wants* to know them. He's not a God who is irritated by their continual requests for forgiveness or preoccupied with other things when he is needed the most.

He is there. He is open to *our* cries, and he listens to *us*.

He has grace for us.

He doesn't simply tolerate our need for second and third chances; he doesn't begrudgingly make a way for our repentance. Instead, he takes pleasure in helping us "turn our hearts back again." He will move mountains and call down fire and trust us *one more time*, even when our track record would make any sensible person do the opposite.

God is not skeptical.

God believes in us, and grace is his way of demonstrating it.

God will be defined not by his anger toward us but rather by his kindness toward us. He's more kind than we ever imagined him to be.

Even when God seems absent, and even when life's serenity is shattered by sudden tragedy, even when our prayers seem to be deflected by the wall of our unrighteousness, God is never far away.

This God doesn't have to be asked twice.

He has already decided to answer . . . even before we ask.

Because he is a God of grace.

THREE

THE GOD WITH DIRTY HANDS

S OME PEOPLE HAVE A PROBLEM WITH GRACE because it makes God seem weak to them. It humanizes him. It doesn't exactly fit our image of the divine God sitting on his throne with a scepter and a gavel and a voice that thunders like dynamite.

We like to think of God as far away from us—like a famous person we admire but don't really know. We kind of keep track of what's happening in his story, but surely he doesn't know much about ours, and if he does, he doesn't care to know more.

He's in heaven, after all—busy doing other things, like lightning and thunder and stuff like that.

Maybe we like this way of thinking because it makes it easier for us to ignore him when *we* want to assume his role of rule maker in our own lives. Or maybe it's just been reinforced by too many caricatures on too many movie screens. Regardless, it causes us to miss the beauty of his grace.

The truth is that God is close to us, but his nearness doesn't make him any less powerful. He's *GOD*, but he's also with us somehow in life, with all of its messes and topsy-turvies.

The Bible teaches us that God "demonstrates his own love for us" (Rom. 5:8) in how he came to us in Jesus. He didn't expect us to climb up to him. He climbed down to us. He got his hands dirty so that we could have our hearts cleaned.

And by that example, he taught us a great deal about God's character. By studying Jesus' life, we find hints about God's heart—and therefore we find hints about how we should go about living our own lives.

THE LEPER COLONY

It was in a leper colony in India that, finally, I really began to understand Jesus' incarnation.

I'll never forget standing there at the door of the village with a bag of oranges, trying to persuade the gatekeeper to let me into his leper colony. I was starting to get a little nervous. My friends in India had warned me that this particular village of leprosy victims had a tendency to get a little testy sometimes, and I should enter with extreme caution lest I cause a scene.

This, *of course*, was why I brought a bag of oranges. My friends had reiterated this advice as if it were just common sense: you take oranges to people with leprosy. "Duh, Johnnie—everyone knows this."

Apparently, even for people inflicted with leprosy, the stomach is the shortest route to the heart, so there I was, with my oranges, trying my hardest to persuade this man to let me inside.

I hadn't told my parents that I was visiting a group of lepers who had been exiled from their community because of their highly contagious, flesh-eating, eventually fatal disease. I'd felt it was safer to simply tell them I was going on a little excursion outside of town. They had attended enough Sunday school classes to understand the sheer terror evoked by the word *leprosy.*

So had I.

My plan was to e-mail them after the fact. "So, I visited a leper colony today," I would say, and then move on to other things.

My dad is from the southern United States, so I had to be careful how I handled this. He's from a place where people "tote" guns and fight for the honor of their families, and he had assured me that if I ever got "in a pickle" while overseas he was going to "hop on a plane" and "break out the south Georgia redneck on those people." I was a little nervous that my three-hundred-pound dad, who looks suspiciously like a member of the Soprano family, was going to hijack a plane to India and "break out" some Southern-style violence on my newfound, diseased friends if he thought they created any threat to my welfare. This would not be a best-case scenario for a rookie missionary just trying to share the love of Jesus with some sick people.

Two thousand years after Christ, people around the world still have much the same perception of this most feared of all diseases as they did when Jesus walked the earth. Leprosy still conjures up images of men and women with decaying fingers and noses, bandaged from head to toe, as they lurch toward a tortuously slow death.

ENTERING THE COLONY

Before long, I had bargained my way through the gate of the colony and discovered exactly what I had expected. It was something out of a movie reel produced in a different time, when this sort of thing was more commonplace.

There were two or three dozen makeshift homes crammed within the small walls of this musty complex, and each shack sheltered a man or woman who looked like they had been plucked right out of the first century. Their open sores were held together by bloodstained bandages, many of their appendages had been sanded down into irritated nubs, and their noses had been ground down to the point that they were almost totally flat—two holes in their faces through which they could barely draw each difficult breath.

Seeing leprosy alive and well was the pinnacle of culture shock for me as a sheltered American college student. It rattled me from the inside out. It was traumatizing. I had no idea that people on planet Earth were still suffering this way, especially in a time when leprosy can be largely eliminated if people are educated enough to know how to get the right treatment as quickly as possible.

The experience was an emotional earthquake.

I felt a deep, powerful compassion for these dear people, but if I'm to be totally honest, I was also repelled by their wounds. My heart was broken, but I was also concerned for my own health, and I didn't give all of myself because I was so afraid I wouldn't be able to leave the suffering behind when I left that barricaded colony.

I don't like admitting that I wasn't some prepackaged American version of Mother Teresa who swept in and ignored the bandages and the blood and the smell. I wasn't that gentle and warm and caring. I was deeply moved—but not moved enough to put my inhibitions aside and "get my hands dirty." I was afraid there was such a thing as *too* dirty.

It was uncomfortable to learn that day, bag of oranges in hand in the home of lepers, that I had far less grace than Jesus. I would have never done for those people what Jesus did for me. Jesus didn't just climb down the stairs to planet Earth to walk around in a leper colony. It was as if he became a leper himself, taking all the pain and putrid sin of history and consuming it in one big gulp on the cross.

JESUS: THE KING OF KINGS
AND LOVER OF LEPERS

The way Jesus himself interacted with leprosy victims is a great illustration of God's compassion for us.

Actually, Jesus lived in a highly superstitious time, when most people believed that leprosy was the result of a curse or of some incorrigible and hidden sin—not unlike modern Eastern religious systems that teach that your current place in life is the direct result of the karma, or lack thereof, in your previous life. It's also not unlike the bad advice that Job, the Bible's iconic figure of suffering, received from his nice, "godly" friends when they barked at him to repent before his sin caused even more problems.

In first-century culture, and especially among the ultra-religious elite, a victim of leprosy was often believed to have been afflicted by God. His disease resulted from some sin, attitude, or choice that deserved *just* punishment, and one of God's chief tools for administering such justice was the infliction of this debilitating, humiliating, and miserable disease. It was the application of the age-old *law of retribution*—bad things happen to bad people.

So anyone—even well-to-do people and sophisticated, religious, respected members of society—unfortunate enough to "catch" this disease would immediately be banished from society, condemned to a life of shame.

Should a leprosy victim ever have to travel back into town, he would have to announce himself as he walked through the streets, hands covering his upper lip: "Unclean, unclean, unclean!" In fact, even in recent history, in some parts of the world lepers have been required to carry a bell to warn others in the streets that they were approaching.

Leprosy, above all things, produced fear—and not the simple startlement of finding a spider crawling across your shoulder. This was incapacitating, panic-inducing fear. If you were walking down a market street with your kids, and you heard the hoarse cry of "unclean" from an approaching leper, you would immediately, without hesitation, drop everything you were doing to get you and your family as far away from the approaching leper as quickly as possible. Most modern people can't comprehend the kind of terror that leprosy produced.

This cultural context is essential to understanding why Jesus' interaction with lepers was so absolutely startling, and such a potent demonstration of the length to which God will go to extend grace even to people whom society believes are the least deserving of it.

But then, isn't that the definition of grace?

Jesus was often observed in conversations with prostitutes and tax collectors just after giving a cold shoulder to the wheeling-and-dealing Sadducees or refusing to get in a ceremonial tiff with the always-arguing Pharisees. But fooling around with leprosy victims went far beyond even that. These were the people despised by the most despised people in society. Even the greedy tax collectors wouldn't dare get close enough to extort the lepers. And lepers were too disgusting for the prostitutes to sell them their services.

Even Jesus' disciples thought his interaction with lepers was reckless—even dangerous.

Yet, almost as quickly as we're introduced to Jesus in the gospel of Mark, we find him running into a man with leprosy.

His reaction is a showstopper.

Jesus didn't run away, turn his head, or try to avoid the diseased man.

No doubt the man had yelled "unclean" as he entered the city of Capernaum in a desperate effort to seek out the new rabbi who was rumored to have the powers to heal even leprosy.

When Jesus saw the man, the Bible says he was "filled with compassion" (Mark 1:41 NIV 1984). *Filled* means just that. He was topped off, almost pouring over with compassion.

He was *moved*, as some other translations have put it. When Jesus saw this rejected, isolated, abused, and very sick man, he was immediately moved from somewhere deep inside to care about this man. It was his first and immediate reaction. Most people were *immediately* repulsed, should they be unfortunate enough to stumble upon a leper. Jesus *immediately* cared for him.

Then Jesus did something absolutely absurd. The Bible says, in Mark 1:41, "Jesus reached out his hand and touched the man" (NIV 1984).

Another author has imagined the emotion of a moment when Jesus met a leper, from the perspective of the leper:

> He [Jesus] stopped and looked in my direction as did dozens of others. A flood of fear swept across the crowd. Arms flew in front of faces. Children ducked behind parents. "Unclean!"

someone shouted. Again, I don't blame them. I was a huddled mass of death. But I scarcely heard them. I scarcely saw them. Their panic I'd seen a thousand times. His compassion, however, I'd never beheld. Everyone stepped back except him. He stepped toward me. *Toward* me.

Five years ago my wife had stepped toward me. She was the last to do so. Now he did. I did not move. I just spoke. "Lord, you can heal me if you will." Had he healed me with a word, I would have been thrilled. Had he cured me with a prayer, I would have rejoiced. But he wasn't satisfied with speaking to me. He drew near me. He *touched* me. Five years ago my wife had touched me. No one had touched me since. Until today.[1]

The touch of Jesus was all it took to yank this man out of his misery and re-create his story. Within seconds, the leper's life course was totally altered one more time.

When hopeless situations come face-to-face with Jesus, things change, and this leper's life was changed forever.

Jesus' touch activated something inside of that man, and it must have produced one massive biological fireworks display. Can you imagine the chemical reaction as that man's predicament met the power of his Creator? There were probably sparks flying off of his DNA in every direction as twisted things straightened and numb things were resuscitated and life infused death to make something beautiful again out of this man whose days had been numbered. It was the moment where this man's soul heard the voice of his Creator again, and the miraculous stepped into the inevitable and made a dying man dance.

Jesus was a healer, but he wasn't *just* a healer—he was the healer who used his very hands to catalyze his miracles. And we see Jesus doing this all through the Gospels—at least five times in the book of Mark alone. Jesus willingly, frequently touched the men and women others tried to avoid. He not only interacted with these rejected ones. He reached out and *touched* them.

He wanted, and was willing, to be close to them. That closeness was not the sign of a weak God who meddled with the undeserving, but of a strong God who could heal the sick and perform an even greater miracle: giving dignity back to the despised.

Grace and God's power are friends, not enemies, of one another. It is not a weak God who associates with weak people, but rather a strong God, attracted to the opportunity to be powerful in their weakness.

Grace is hard. It shows not God's weakness, but his incredible strength.

THE GOD WHO DIRTIES HIS HANDS

Grace is the word we use to describe the means by which God allows people to overcome their differences and become close again, and Jesus demonstrated this grace by touching the leper.

Touching someone is an automatic sign of intimacy. It is often tender, compassionate; it is a bridge not just from a hand to a shoulder but also from a heart to a heart. You touch people you care about. You touch people you like. You touch people when they need to know that someone cares about them. When your friend gets a tragic midnight call, and she comes running to you seeking comfort, what do you do? You give her a shoulder to cry on, right? You don't dole out calibrated answers to her hard questions about the unfairness of life. You don't tell her that you "understand what she's going through."

You do one simple thing.

You execute the power of touch.

You put your arm around her as she weeps on your shoulder, so that if she knows nothing else, she at least knows that someone cares about her.

Jesus didn't keep his distance from the messy world that he descended into when he left heaven's golden streets for earth's dusty Middle Eastern villages, filled to capacity with the poor and frustrated, the disenfranchised and the rejected. Jesus didn't revel in his priceless glory—rather, he gave himself completely to the opportunity to make the inglorious feel that they mattered to God.

He "made himself of no reputation, and took upon him the form of a servant," and he intentionally reached out and touched those whom society rejected (Phil. 2:7 KJV). In fact, to Jesus, the ones respected by society were often the dirty ones. It wasn't the lepers and the prostitutes and the tax collectors who disgusted Jesus. It was the religious elites, the politically empowered, the rich and the powerful.

The Pharisees had no excuse—they were the guardians of the truth, but they had long traded a love for truth for a love for power. Jesus *expected* those whom society deemed "sinners" to live like "sinners," but he must have been so disappointed to find that those who had memorized the Torah were blind to their own pride and self-righteousness. They needed God's grace as much as the sinners they wanted to stone.

Jesus cared little about impressing the important people. He was too busy getting his hands messy with the regular ones, and he didn't need friends in high places to change the world. In fact, eventually, those in high places would murder him, and by doing so, unintentionally and unknowingly, save the world.

Amazingly, Jesus' grace would be kind and strong enough to provide forgiveness—even to them.

FOUR

JESUS MADE A MESS OF THINGS

IT'S HIS GRACE THAT MAKES JESUS UNIQUE, and it was the implications of his grace that caused so many people to miss him altogether.

There are plenty of wishy-washy, sort-of-religious people who preach that all spiritual roads eventually converge on the same path toward God. Jesus is just another version of a remarkably similar idea of "god" or of a "savior" that weaves its way through all the religions of the world.

Jesus isn't unique to them. He's just one potato in a bushel. Jesus is just the Christian version of Shiva or Buddha or Muhammad.

But there are also plenty of people who believe that Jesus is actually unique, and that his uniqueness is most evident in the notion of grace. To fully understand the everyday implications of grace in our lives, it's helpful to understand how it was exhibited in Jesus' own everyday life.

Actually, Jesus' life was unique—even strange—right from the beginning.

GOD WITH US

Everyone was expecting the Messiah to come with fireworks.

But Jesus plopped down to earth in the most unorthodox way. Rather than assigning his angels to announce his arrival to the rich and powerful, and rather than sending a delegation ahead to prepare every detail of his arrival, Jesus showed up in near total obscurity.

The angels made their announcement to shepherds and Eastern philosophers, and completely ignored the Pharisees, the Sadducees, the king, and the Roman emperor.

The gateway by which God entered planet Earth was the womb of a teenage mother from a tiny, backward village, and when Jesus was born he was forced to breathe his first breath within a musty, smelly feeding trough.

Think about that. Jesus' first breath of air on the planet that he created was seasoned with a hint of manure and of old, dry hay.

Herod, the king of the Jews, heard about Jesus' arrival only by a rumor, and the Romans didn't know that God himself had arrived within their eastern provinces—and didn't care one way or the other until he began to cause trouble.

Jesus is the God who comes to us without fanfare. He seems weak when he arrives in that manger, but he's anything but weak. He's powerful enough to hold back his glory as he begins his journey of wading through the muck of man's sin, and all the way to the cross, he demonstrates that the values of the kingdom of God are different from the values of this world, or of the Romans or the Pharisees or Herod himself. Jesus taught that it was *by grace* that you enter into this new way of living and this renewed relationship with God.

When you think about it, the whole story really is absurd.

Gods are primarily thought of as "powerful"—like Zeus with his lightning bolt. They don't waste their time meddling in the lives of humans. They're too busy being gods.

And Jesus *is* all-powerful. Jesus can hold the universe, which he created, in the palm of his hand. Even so, Jesus comes to us totally differently from any other god. He entered history as a God who looked more like man.

Jesus didn't care about impressing the barons and the politicians. He didn't have time for the rabbis with their long prayers and outward adornments.

Jesus came for everyone, and especially for those who didn't deserve God's attention.

He came for the regular men and women who claw and fight their way through life, trying to make this world a little better place. He came fully aware of man's inadequacies, and he didn't intend to rub them in.

He came not to judge the sin of the world but rather to take onto his own shoulders the burden of giving a second chance to people who didn't deserve one.

Jesus didn't just send a message to man through yet another prophet. Instead, he dropped a staircase from heaven so that he can walk with us, touch us, talk to us, feel like we feel, hurt as we hurt, struggle as we struggle, and eventually help us get to where we ought to be—in the presence of God again.

He handles us with care. He relishes the opportunity to make something beautiful out of our messes.

He arrived on the scene with a certain everydayness. When you imagine him there in the feeding trough in Bethlehem, you could almost miss that this was a moment of such cosmic importance—a time when God grabbed history in his two hands and ripped it apart.

Jesus' arrival was, in fact, the *most* significant moment in all of history, and it was his *grace* that brought him here, and his grace that defined the revolutionary way he taught us to think about God and his kingdom.

You would think that the wonderful news of God's grace would be received with open arms. But grace, like a glimmering diamond, shimmers most brightly when it's placed squarely on something dark as night.

Jesus arrived with a great gift—a gift that almost no one wanted.

JESUS THE RADICAL

Jesus was not popular. He was misunderstood, reviled, and ridiculed, and some really influential people hated him with the kind of hatred we reserve for the Hitlers of this world. It was the power of his grace that kept Jesus from holding grudges against his enemies and that somehow allowed him to eventually offer salvation to them as well.

And he had *lots* of enemies.

He was a threat to the political and religious institutions of the first century, and by the end of his time on earth, his mere presence would evoke such passionate emotion that even sophisticated religious leaders would find themselves plotting murder with the types of people they wouldn't come within a mile of under normal circumstances. The much-maligned Herodians were plotting together with the Pharisees, the Bible tells us (Mark 3:6). The Herodians were Jewish allies of the Roman Empire. The Pharisees hated both the Herodians and the Romans because they were convinced that those two groups were conspiring together to defile the Jewish holy land. That meant that the Herodians, to the Pharisees, were even worse than the Romans because they were traitors. And yet Jesus was so reviled by the Pharisees that they were willing to swallow their pride (which they had much of) and lower themselves to plotting with the Herodians to ensure his demise.

They hated him mainly because Jesus' unorthodox teachings about the kingdom of God were an affront to their own. Jesus threatened their power, deliberately confronting their corruption of faith and tearing down the walls they had built between God and man.

Jesus was grieved by how they had allowed the temple to be turned into a massive, commercial racket. The religious leaders were swindlers who took advantage of the devotion of the Jewish people for their own personal and financial gain. Many, and maybe most, of the rabbis were drunk on their authority, and despite spending their entire lives studying the Jewish law and prophets, almost none of them noticed when the actual Messiah showed up on their doorstep. The "church" was full of hypocrites, and having Jesus in town made their hypocrisy stand out starkly in the Judean sun.

Most of all, Jesus hated how the religious leaders had made it more and more difficult for the people God loved to know that God loved them. The religious leaders had buried fellowship with God behind so many walls of religious ritual and man-made law that instead of helping people get close to God, they spent their lives reminding people of how far away from him they were.

But before you get too critical of the Pharisees . . . many of us would have been skeptical of Jesus ourselves.

I mean—he was *asking* for it. He said radical things that provoked all kinds of reactions. Imagine, for instance, what nationalistic Jews would have thought when Jesus preached that soon the Jewish temple would be pummeled to gravel. If you had been a Jew, you might have tried running him out of town too.

But sometimes, radical messages are the right ones, and Jesus was spot-on. He told people the truth, whether they liked it or not, and he told it to everyone, rich and poor alike. Within a half generation of Jesus' resurrection, the Jewish temple *was* destroyed by the Romans.

At the time he predicted it, the people hadn't believed him. But he was so convinced of it that he sat upon the Mount of Olives, looking over the glorious temple, and began to weep over the future fate of his beloved Jerusalem.

He wept.

That's grace showing up again.

He didn't point his finger at the city and scream his prediction with the harsh rhetoric of a judgmental preacher. He didn't walk up and down the interstate with a cardboard sign, declaring God's coming wrath.

His justice was delivered through his tears.

He absolutely loved these people, even as they denied him.

DIFFICULT FOR JESUS

The doctrine of the incarnation reminds us that Jesus was both divine *and* human. His humanity endured enormous stress as he was repeatedly rejected by the very people he came to love. It hurt.

In fact, on the eve of his arrest we find Jesus so distressed over what was coming that he collapsed in an olive grove, weeping, under such duress that he perspired drops of blood.

It was heartbreaking for Jesus. The purpose of his trip to earth was to give *grace* to people, but so many people rejected, or were indifferent to, the good news he brought.

Because Jesus wasn't the kind of Savior people were expecting, he was rejected by most, and the few who accepted him were mainly from the other side of the tracks.

Jesus was considered *edgy* by the religious establishment. He was an antiestablishment heretic who ignored certain "sacred" Jewish practices. He did his own thing, often in blatant defiance of the most respected religious leaders.

Jesus wasn't the kind of revolutionary one might have expected to make history. He didn't manipulate the crowds or pull together coalitions, gathering as much power as possible. In fact, he ignored the systems of power that made the ancient world function.

Yet grace was ever present in his life and ministry, even in his relationships with his enemies. Jesus wasn't so much angry at the religious establishment as he was heartbroken over their unbelief—so much so that he once broke down as he approached Jerusalem. Looking down over the city from a high hill, he said, "If you only knew . . ." (Luke 19:42 GNT).

Choosing to follow Jesus wasn't a respectable, admirable thing to do. Following Jesus was truly radical. It would cost you—and it might cost you everything.

It was like wearing a Red Sox cap in the middle of Yankee Stadium. It was a provocation.

———

And why did Jesus go through all of this? Why did he knowingly invite so much ridicule and shame, so much pain and embarrassment? Why was he willing to start life in a feeding trough, only so he could end it by being cursed at, flogged, stripped of his clothes, and nailed to an executioner's cross? Why did he leave the Father's side and exit heaven to wander around this heartsick place?

He did all of this for one reason: you.

That's right—*you.*

He caught your eye through history's window as he stared over the banister of heaven, and he determined that he would care for you and give you a chance. He would make grace available and give you an opportunity to enjoy peace again.

And maybe you already know all of this. But I'm wondering if you *really* know it.

Like a lover catching a first glance of his beloved in a crowded train station after a long journey back home from a faraway land, Jesus caught your eye and then endured the cross so that you might be invited to dine again with God.

Into a culture where the gods seemed to look, and behave, like superhumans with perfect physiques and Herculean qualities—came Jesus. The *one true God* didn't come adorned with Romanesque glory, and he didn't arrive to a celebration in a city like Rome or Athens, Alexandria or Jerusalem. He arrived in Bethlehem, and he came as an innocent child.

Jesus went through hell to show us kindness, to give us grace. He was on a mission to woo back God's long, lost love.

Us.

FIVE

JESUS AND THE REJECTS

JESUS WOULD RATHER NOT EVEN GO TO Jerusalem. It was chaos.

He much preferred more normal places with more normal people. He left more of his grace in those places than he did in the bigger cities.

Actually, other than fulfilling the cultural necessity of attending Jewish festivals and events, Jesus largely ignored Jerusalem. He spent far more time in the idyllic hills surrounding the Sea of Galilee. The big-city folk in Jerusalem would have looked down on Jesus as a peasant who liked peasant sorts of places with peasant sorts of people.

Jesus wasn't the cocktail-party type.

He was the son-of-a-carpenter type.

The folks who shopped on fancy streets wouldn't have given him a passing glance.

Jesus wore painter's pants, not Prada.

When Jesus did go to Jerusalem, it was a disturbing and difficult experience for him. The religious and political leaders would often incite arguments with him, and the commercialization of the temple seemed to drive him mad. Eventually, Jesus just bulldozed over it all, turning over the money-changing tables and making a royal mess fitting for the front page of the *Jerusalem Post*.

In all likelihood, many people thought he was totally insane.

Jesus wasn't the kind of messiah who fit into the box. Most people were expecting a political messiah who would drive out the Roman occupiers, a savior who would play politics with the Pharisees and Sadducees, and a revolutionary who would set up a new kingdom in defiance of Roman rule. They expected a militant savior who would be impossible for the great Roman Empire to defeat.

Jesus instead liked to help sick people, loved playing with children, hated to pander to the politicians, and didn't much care what the people who "mattered the most" thought of him.

According to Jesus' own words, these powerful leaders were nothing but "whitewashed tombs" (Matt. 23:27). They were sons of Satan and "wolves" (Matt. 7:15). They were out to get him at every turn and in every possible way, and the tension was so high that when a Pharisee named Nicodemus actually did want to meet with Jesus, he scheduled a clandestine conversation in the middle of the night (John 3) so as to not draw attention to his encounter with such an "extremist."

And that's exactly how they viewed the Son of God—as an extremist.

———

Things always came to a head at the temple.

The temple sat like a crown atop Zion's hill in Jerusalem. It was a place of deep historic and spiritual importance for all Jewish people, including Jesus. But it was also a very difficult place for him. Everything that was good about Judaism and everything that was horrible about it had collided in that place and in that international city. In some sense it was the epicenter of a war that was raging in the hearts of the Jewish people. When Jesus came to Jerusalem he was stepping onto the front lines of that war.

This is one of the reasons Jesus found deep solace in the quiet northern plains of Israel. It was here that he felt most at home, not in the bustling, cosmopolitan, dog-eat-dog world of Jerusalem.

For one thing, Nazareth, the city of Jesus' childhood, sat in those northern plains. His dear mom and his father's carpentry shop were there too. It was where his momma had cooked the meals of his childhood, where his first friendships were made, and where numerous parties and weddings and festivals went reveling into the night. Nazareth was where Jesus could let his hair down and be as human as he liked.

Nazareth was a world away from the bustling metropolis of Jerusalem. The population of the village probably maxed out at about four hundred people, and everyone knew each other. Nazareth's size and insignificance were probably what prompted one critic of Jesus' teaching to say, "Isn't this the carpenter's son? Isn't his mother's name Mary, and aren't his brothers James, Joseph, Simon and Judas? Aren't all his sisters with us? Where then did this man get all these things?"

The critic, the Bible says, "took offense at him."[1]

Why?

He was from Nazareth.

Jesus was a "small-town" type of guy who seemed much more comfortable in the tranquil rhythm of a fishing village around the Sea of Galilee, or observing his father's carpentry, than in the cacophony of the big city. He wasn't a big-city type of guy with designer clothes and a trendy lifestyle bent on impressing people. Jesus never wanted to be a celebrity. He was a boy from the rural north, and the privileged of Jerusalem weren't too impressed with the children of working-class people from Nazareth—*of all places*.

Jesus didn't meet the profile of an up-and-coming Jewish prophet either. In fact, Nazareth was so unimpressive that when Nathanael was invited by Philip to meet Jesus, he replied, "[He's from] Nazareth! Can anything good come from there?"[2]

It's a fascinating mystery that when God scanned the earth to find the place where Jesus would grow up, he chose a carpenter's home in a typical Middle Eastern village. He didn't zero in on an epicenter of power or of influence. He didn't make Jesus the golden child of the aristocrats. Nope, the King of kings grew up in a simple home, eating village food, and living a village life in near obscurity.

Perhaps if a caravan of Roman or Jewish leaders had seen the young Jesus playing on the side of the road, they would have assumed that he would never amount to much. He would have been underestimated and ignored.

Meanwhile, that boy Jesus had the power to shut off the sun and melt Mount Everest. He could have turned the Mediterranean into a boiling pot of lava, and he could have, with a passing thought, made the great Roman cities crumble into dust so fine that a gust of wind could have blown them into the sea.

This little Jewish boy was the most formidable person on planet Earth, not only at that time but for all time. But he chose to live the life of a regular man.

Jesus chose to be the "not good enough" Messiah because he was especially interested in the "not good enoughs."

MINISTRY *AMONG* THE PEOPLE

Jesus probably had a small-town accent too. Maybe it's because he didn't like the hassle of going into the city that he focused most of his ministry on the villages.

It was there that he dined with the blue-collar folk who knew how to work in the old-fashioned way, and it was there that Jesus found almost all of his closest associates. In obscure places, he performed most of his miracles and delivered his most profound teachings.

Jesus' parables and his revolutionary interpretation of the Hebrew Scriptures were often spoken for the first time directly into the hearts of villagers (probably illiterate) living in and around the Sea of Galilee. The religious elite would never have cast their own "pearls" before such "swine," but Jesus took great pride in giving to lowly people what others thought they didn't deserve.

It was grace that marked his ministry.

It was grace also that allowed people like Peter, John, Matthew, and Simon to become his closest associates. Rather than scouring the nation to recruit the best and brightest young rabbis to become coveted members of the Messiah's elite core of disciples, Jesus instead looked in Galilee. He almost entirely avoided overly fervent career students of the Bible. Instead, he recruited working-class fishermen, a tax collector, and even a member of a radical, leftist political party that was inclined toward terrorism if it would accomplish the ousting of Rome from Israel (Simon *the Zealot*).

It was Jesus' grace that inspired him to recruit such novices to play an essential part in his plan to change the world.

Disciples of leading rabbis were required to be among the most educated young people in the nation. The leading rabbis would carefully select their apprentices from the cream of the crop. They would comb through the synagogue's enrollment lists to find Jerusalem's up-and-coming leaders. Once they found promising disciples, they would recruit them early and work for years to mold them into future biblical scholars.

They selected graduates from the "Ivy League." A disciple of a rabbi was probably from a good family, known to be intelligent, and most likely wealthy and influential already.

Jesus' chosen disciples hadn't even made it to community college. They would have flunked rabbinical school, for sure, and some of them probably had.

They were tradesmen with calloused hands and farmer's tans. They were *tough* like coal miners or steel workers, like my own great-uncle who spent his entire working life running cranes that loaded barges. They had oil on their clothes and wore overalls and could arm-wrestle the best of 'em, though they'd never lifted a dumbbell.

This is, to me, one of the most remarkable things about Jesus.

He recruited everyday people to change history.

He didn't care what people thought of him or his ragtag group of rookie preachers. Jesus somehow knew that fishermen might make the best fishers of men, and a former tax collector would make it very clear that no one lives outside of the parameters of the grace of God. It was somehow commonsense to Jesus that normal people would be more apt to reach normal people. Jesus was illustrating to us that the kingdom was for everyone, not just the best ones.

From the very beginning, grace made Jesus' faith a populist movement.

It didn't begin in the ivory tower. It began on the cul-de-sac.

GRACE IS FOR THE REST OF US, NOT JUST THE BEST OF US

But we don't think of contemporary Christianity this way, do we?

Christianity is for those who are either (1) better than us or (2) naturally inclined toward religion.

In other words, many of us believe that Christianity is for people who have their stuff together *already*, and most of us don't have our stuff together. We fight to do our own thing, while at the same time knowing that we *need* God desperately in our lives, and inability to win this battle causes us to lose patience with ourselves and our faith. Sometimes, when we listen to preachers who know the Bible "like the back of their hand," we feel intimidated about our own lack of Bible knowledge. We don't know the names and the places. We can't pronounce the words, and sometimes, if we're honest, we don't even find the Bible that interesting.

Like Jesus' disciples, we're interested—but we're always betraying our ignorance.

Then, of course, we have our bad habits, our habitual sins, our bad attitudes and loose tempers. We *want* to stop smoking or stop having sex or stop shooting up or stop worshipping our money or ourselves—we just never quite succeed. We can't imagine that Jesus would be interested in us until we dust ourselves off a bit, until we get our closets all cleaned out and our sins under control and become the kind of person who can pronounce the name *Methuselah* properly and actually remember who he was and why he mattered.

Christianity is for other people.

Better people.

Not us regular people.

It's for people who are holier than we are, more devoted to God. People who have their lives under control—and especially if they have a peculiar fascination with ancient history and literature.

This prevailing sense of spiritual inadequacy is epidemic within Christian culture. It's one of the greatest barriers standing between our faith and those who are curious about it. So many people feel that even despite their best intentions a committed faith is just beyond them. They aren't disciple material. They're too rough around the edges; they have calluses on their hands or weights on their shoulders or deep, dark secrets hiding in the shadowed corners of their hearts. They're not smart enough or holy enough or good enough or interested enough for God to want them within his elite core of followers. Plus, they have jobs. They have to catch the fish to feed their families, or sign up enough clients, or win their political races. They're not preachers or missionaries or scholars. So they assume Jesus wouldn't have time for them.

Most Christians aren't Pharisee material. They're more like regular people, like fishermen or tax collectors.

They fear that they'll never be "holy." They need lots of grace.

And in the middle of all this frustration, Jesus comes to us and says, "You're *welcome* into the kingdom of God. Just trust me and follow me, and you're in."

———

This is what makes the gospel such "good news," and this is exactly what made Jesus' message so powerful that, once people really grasped it, it became the most significant religious movement in history.

Jesus wasn't interested in creating Pharisees. He was interested in people like you and me. He came with lots of grace, because he knew we needed it.

He is the kind of savior who ushers in history's greatest moment from a feed trough with shepherds on the front row. He's the odd kind of king who chooses to live his early life among the regular people in a tiny, poor, and insignificant place like Nazareth, rather than the ritzy glamour of Rome or Athens. When he could have sat at tables eating fine food with princes, he chose instead to eat fish cooked over an open fire, eating with people who used to have leprosy, or beggars, or tax collectors who had been seduced by money—just as the religious leaders had been seduced by their self-righteousness, pride, and lust for power.

Jesus is the kind of teacher who loved to throw his pearls of wisdom to the people others thought neither deserved it nor knew what to do with it. Jesus, instead, seemed to think that only people who knew how much they needed the grace of God would truly appreciate receiving it.

Jesus is the kind of spiritual leader who loves—who, in fact, is obsessed by—those of us who are a little rough around the edges. His mission wasn't to those who already have their stuff together—it was to those who simply *wanted* to have their stuff together, and who knew they needed a lot of grace and a lot of help to get there.

Jesus opened the gate of heaven wide for anyone who wanted in, and he was just fine with those who stumbled a few times on the path to holiness.

He came as a patient spiritual guide who didn't expect his patients to heal themselves. He knew they needed him, and he was glad to be there for them.

I NEED GOD

Many of us stumble into Jesus' emergency room when we're already losing buckets of blood.

Life gets hard and we run out of options, or maybe we just get curious about faith again, or we simply can't find any other way to fix our problems. So we check ourselves in to Jesus' rehab center, frantically and desperately knocking on the door of Dr. Jesus in the middle of the night.

We don't feel good enough.

We don't feel adequate.

We don't feel that God has any reason to pay attention to us.

But suddenly we've reached the end of our options, so we pray, we plead, we cry, and we beg for him to pay attention to us and to help us in our crisis.

And what do we find at the door of Dr. Jesus?

We find grace.

Even though we thought we were completely off his radar screen, he was paying attention to us all along. In fact, he left his light on in expectation of our midnight call.

While we thought he was spending all his time with the preachers and the rabbis and the man from our church who prays five hours a day, Jesus was actually following *us* around with a bucketful of grace, ready to trust us one more time.

What's tragic is that the same grace was available to us all along, even when our worlds weren't falling apart, even when we thought we had other options. We were so convinced that God needed us to get our lives together *first* that we just couldn't see it.

Herein we find a great paradox.

In the story of Jesus, we find that the greatest recipients of his grace are those who needed it the most and who thought they deserved it the least. The religious elite, who thought they *deserved* the grace and favor of God, were those who would miss it altogether.

SIX

GRACE SLEEPS WITH TRUTH

GRACE IS FREE AND IT'S LIBERAL. BUT IT should not be abused. It's meant to be a first step into a new and liberated life where man and God are friends again. It's the key that unlocks the secret of how man was made to live. It was never intended to be a license to live selfishly.

This is why Jesus appears to us as more than just a purveyor of grace. He is also a prophet who preaches truth that stings. He was kind and liberal with his grace, but he didn't come to us preaching pretty little self-help sermons that simply made people feel better about themselves.

Jesus' grace paved a path to God's best plan for man's life, which involved living in a way appropriate for a citizen of God's kingdom. In that sense, his teaching was sometimes more akin to a battering ram than a Styrofoam bat. He cut to the chase, made his point in blunt terms, and was more than happy to point out the elephant in the room that everyone else would have preferred to ignore. Jesus spoke frankly to the issues that were off-limits, and that were, for that very reason, souring faith from the inside out.

Jesus' liberality with grace wasn't an end in itself. It was a door to a new life lived as God had designed life to be lived.

But as I read the Bible, Jesus wasn't, even at his most prophetic, one of those loud, angry preachers, one of those in-your-face communicators who wielded guilt like a javelin. He spoke with grace. He was sly like a serpent and gentle as a dove. He would look you in the eye and whisper something that no one else knew. He could say the right thing in exactly the right way to let you know immediately when something was out of balance in your life.

There's a wonderful illustration of this in the account of Jesus' recruitment of Nathanael to be among his disciples.

The first time they met, even before they'd been introduced, Jesus called him by name, and Nathanael replied, "How do you know me?"

Jesus said, "I saw you while you were still under the fig tree before Philip called you."[1]

Here's what's interesting. We have no idea what Nathanael was doing, or thinking about, under that mysterious fig tree. Maybe he was praying or doubting or waiting for something. Maybe he was considering ending his life; maybe he was asking himself some great, soul-searching question. We have no idea, but *Jesus knew* exactly what was going on under that fig tree. And it was something of such significance, something so private and unknowable, that Nathanael replied immediately, "Rabbi, you are the Son of God; you are the king of Israel."[2]

See, there are two kinds of prophets.

There are the prophets who stand on street corners and scream at the top of their lungs. They protest and wave banners and interrupt press conferences and shout down those who disagree with them. They are brash, and they believe that if they are loud enough and aggressive enough, then people will believe.

People will change, and the world will conform. We've all met these folks; they tend to carry big Bibles and put their fingers in our faces. They're always ready to point out a pile of sins we've been neglecting, and they use guilt like a sledgehammer to batter us into holiness.

Then there are the prophets who minister courageously, but do so with grace. Instead of shouting, they can whisper the right word at the right time in the right way, and it's like a knife that cuts us to the core of our being. Rather than tuning out their messages, we *hear* them, and they cause us to search our ways and change our lives. Jesus was this type of prophet. He would go for the jugular, for sure—but he would camouflage his atom bomb in a cute little parable. His words did the job because they were so strategic, not because he was so loud that you couldn't ignore him.

In Nathanael's case, all Jesus had to do was mention the fig tree, almost in passing—but it was *the* fig tree. To Nathanael, that simple sentence had earth-shaking meaning.

When these prophets speak, we suddenly find ourselves totally convinced that this message was from God, and we have to decide whether to receive it or reject it.

Does it take less courage to speak with both grace and truth than it does to stand on the street corner and bellow hard, unpopular truths? No. It takes just as much.

Jesus was extraordinarily courageous. He wasn't passive-aggressive or conflict avoidant, and he didn't begin by politicking or tickling the ears of those he was about to shake up. In fact, he would routinely walk right into the theological lions' den, stare the religious hypocrites in the eyes as he walked right past them, and then, within their hearing, teach their disciples truths that were totally contradictory to what those teachers had been teaching. Jesus mocked their inconsistencies and challenged them that their popular theology was in fact paving a road that led to hell, not to heaven.

Jesus wasn't even discreet about this.

Take, for example, the moment when he said, "Wide is the gate and broad is the road that leads to destruction, and many enter through it. But small is the gate and narrow the road that leads to life, and only a few find it" (Matt. 7:13–14).

Jesus' next sentence demonstrates how overtly antiestablishment this teaching was: "Watch out for false prophets. They come to you in sheep's clothing, but inwardly they are ferocious wolves" (v. 15).

See, the "false prophets" Jesus was referring to weren't metaphorical. They were probably right there, at that moment, conspiring with one another about how they would eventually take care of this troublesome rabbi *for good*. Jesus said this in their hearing. He was unafraid of their power, and he was unabashed in his mission. He had all the grace in the world, but he also spoke truth.

God's grace persuades us to live the truth that God's way is really the best way.

THE GOSPEL TRAUMATIZES HISTORY

The truth of God's grace is so powerful that it literally had the effect of breaking history in half. Jesus' life was of such iconic significance that it required the redefinition of time. It broke history in half. The calendar was traumatized. From the moment Jesus' visit to earth began in Bethlehem, every historical event since has been designated as *Anno Domini* ("in the year of our Lord").

Shouldn't an event this powerful have a transformative effect on our own lives?

The story of Jesus is that when *he* arrives in history, when *he* arrives in a life, when *he* arrives in a synagogue, when *he* arrives at the local well or in your house or your boat, everything changes. Everything changes because Jesus' way is drastically different from every way that came before it.

It is purely, truly revolutionary.

Jesus' arrival was the great pronouncement of the kindness of God, who has chosen to fix this broken world by repairing man's broken relationship with him. And the means by which he has chosen to do so is by free, easy-to-attain, ready-for-the-asking *grace*.

Man would no longer be required to walk a long and arduous and uncertain path toward God. Man would not be subjected to the religious tyranny of the legalists who would condemn us to deeper and deeper levels of guilt.

God, through Jesus, had flung the door wide open to the narrow way.

The Pharisees and religious leaders had taught that their way of self-righteousness *was* actually the narrow way leading to heaven, but in reality their earn-your-way-to-heaven plan was the *wide way*. It was the normal idea of redemption, and every religion in the world taught some version of it.

None of them worked, and it wouldn't work for the Pharisees either.

The truth of grace is that "God's kindness leads you toward repentance" (Rom. 2:4 NIV 1984).

"NOT GUILTY"

What I like best about the narrow way of grace versus the wide way of works is that all along the way are massive billboards that say in every language of the world: "You're not guilty! You're forgiven! You're healed. Things are okay!" The apostle Paul wrote to the baby believers in Rome, the Washington, DC, of his time, "There is now *no condemnation* for those who are in Christ Jesus" (Rom. 8:1, emphasis added).

It's a liberating feeling when you start to understand how Jesus' invitation to salvation, to the narrow way, liberates you from guilt and condemnation and the weight of having to try so hard to become good.

When we start to understand what we have been freed from— that we're *not guilty*, that we're *free*, that we've been *saved*, *rescued*, and *changed*—our lives begin to change, almost automatically. We don't have to be persuaded and convinced and implored and terrified into doing what's right any longer.

Our motivation for listening to God, for living out his truth, is different, and that change makes it easier to do. We no longer struggle to do what's right to try to get enough notches in our belts to show off to Saint Peter at the pearly gates. We do what's right because we actually believe it's best. We do it out of *delight* and not out of *duty*.

For far too long, Satan has convinced us that our faith is a matter of religious duty. I've seen it in the tired faces of a thousand Christian teenagers who sit in church every Sunday with their eyes glazed over. It's on the guilt-laden shoulders of a thousand war-weary pastors who've taught the Scripture line by line without building a bridge between grace and truth, between the mind and the heart. Christianity is a lifestyle of joyful fellowship with a grace-distributing God whose love has drawn us to repentance. It's not a laborious path to a place of perfection that we'll never reach.

Jesus' totally new religious system stood in stark contrast to every other religious system for one astounding reason: it taught that the door to heaven isn't to be found after a long walk down a difficult road of good deeds. Jesus taught a system of faith that began with a door, an easily accessed door, whose toll had already been paid by the blood of Jesus.

Jesus' way to the kingdom is, as Tim Keller, pastor of Redeemer Presbyterian Church in New York City, has said, "a door that leads to a long road, and not a long road that leads to a door."[3]

Jesus believed that *grace* was more powerful, more attractive, and more motivational than *fear* and *judgment*. Truth would be easier lived and more humbly followed if we understood first that God is wooing us to his path by his kindness.

God, as revolutionary as always, took steps to relieve his people of the centuries-old fear of judgment and the law because he knew that only love would be strong enough to persuade them to do what's right and what's best.

God relinquished the power of fear and judgment that undergirds nearly every other religious system in the world. He saw no further advantage in it. Christianity teaches that, at the cross, Jesus fully satisfied God's wrath and judgment, and God, in turn, made fear and guilt irrelevant.

In Jesus, God has taken care of man's misdeeds and indiscretions, and now man can walk with his head high and his shoulders back, knowing *for certain* that the weight of guilt and shame has been assumed and incinerated by the grace and goodness of God.

God has scribbled on the sky, *"You're forgiven!"*

GRACE ACCEPTS YOU AND CAUSES
YOU TO ACCEPT GOD'S TRUTH

Two of Andrea's and my dearest friends spend their lives counseling people, and in our long conversations about life, they've done their share of counseling me.

Cara and Josh have each told me on a number of occasions that one of the greatest and most needed experiences of a human being is *to be fully known, yet fully loved and accepted.*

This internal longing has driven plenty of people mad. Their starved self-esteem has compelled them to prolong unhealthy relationships or lose themselves in others. It has caused others to change their habits and preferences like a chameleon adapting to the environment around it, and it will sometimes cause them to work themselves to death or give away their dignity or embrace a billion kinds of unhealthy behaviors or take different lovers or different jobs or buy nicer things or better bodies or *work and work and work*—on the chance that they might win acceptance.

Meanwhile, God has broken open history and is shouting at us from heaven: "Jesus has died, he has risen, and I accept you because of his sacrifice for you. You are good now. You are saved now. Stop following all these futile paths and follow me! I can be trusted. I know you *and* I love you!"

That's exactly what God gives us through his Son—grace and love and acceptance. He knows us fully, and he loves us just the same.

Many people have a hard time believing this kind of love exists in the world these days. It is almost unheard-of—and the reason it's almost unheard-of is that it has been *our* responsibility to herald the good news that it exists.

Understanding the width and breadth of God's love has two effects.

First, it makes you go nearly mad with gratitude.

Secondly, it hooks your heart, and you find yourself trusting that God's ways are the best ways. You stop fighting against truth and you embrace it. You see God as primarily *kind* and *benevolent,* and you stop seeing him as the cosmic judge who enjoys laying heavy doses of condemnation on people.

In a word, you find yourself *saturated* with his kindness.

SEVEN

MAYBERRY, TSUNAMIS, AND CLEAN AGAIN

OUR TOWN WAS SLEEPY—A LITTLE BIT LIKE A modern Nazareth. It fit snugly into a small valley in the middle of North Carolina's Great Smoky Mountains. There weren't a lot of people living there. The town never made it into the news. And if you drove by too quickly you almost wouldn't notice the tiny houses nestled in groves of trees and perched on the side of hills.

Our pace of life was *real slow* and *real simple*. Like everyone in the Deep South, we drank syrupy iced tea, talked with a syrupy accent, and moved along at a syrupy pace.

Some of the folks in our little town still churned their own butter, shot their own food, sewed their own clothes, and built their own furniture from scratch. New York City might as well have been a town on the other side of Mars. These folks lived life in the old-fashioned way—in fact, living in the western tip of North Carolina was to step back into a more simplistic time.

The people there worked really hard. The local boys had big muscles that made them good football players, but they weren't weight lifters. They had *earned* their muscles throwing hay and herding cattle and getting in fistfights to preserve their family honor. People were rough-and-tumble and ready to "scrap" if someone challenged them. Everyone in a Southern family had to earn his keep.

I didn't quite fit in.

I played in the band.

So there I was at every football game toting a trombone that was double my height, surrounded by behemoths who had been butchering cows the day before.

I have good memories of those years. We went to a good church, Mom and Dad generally got along, and I made some nice friends. I also learned to pray there and learned to read the Bible. I did it almost every night from 9:00 until 9:30, and was taught to do so by a local businessman who taught Sunday school on the side. In some sense, every sermon I preach and every life that has been affected by my speaking or my writing must be credited somehow to that local businessman who taught me how to love and study God's Word.

Life just trickled by there in the Deep South—no fireworks, nothing too interesting, and "nothing to write home about."

That is . . . until the flood.

THE POWER OF WATER

Our little town once sat on a busy trade route through the southeastern United States. Wagon trains would roll through during America's courageous western migration. The trade route curved adjacent to a river through the little valley that our house was squeezed into. The combination of a flat thoroughfare and accessible water made this one of the only routes through the mountains. So it became steadily populated by the types of people who explore and hunt and defend their rights and pioneer in the places where pioneering is hard.

The river that brought the town to life wasn't, in truth, much to brag about, but it was still the most important part of the culture in our tiny city. People fished there and spent their summer vacations splashing around in it. It supplied power to the entire region. My grandpa, a country pastor, even baptized new converts in it. A half dozen times he recounted to me the moment he "lost the big one." It took him and three deacons to lift that grandma back out of the water when her feet slipped off the rocks beneath her.

At normal flow levels, the river ran five feet deep at most and was mainly calm, but the elderly folks in town talked frequently about the fury of this river when it flooded.

Their stories sounded suspicious and exaggerated to me— probably the result of too much sweet tea and fried chicken. Almost every day we drove by the river, and never did I see an indication that there was any threat of the apocalypse squeezed within its narrow banks.

Clearly, the proverbial marbles of these old folks had long been shaken loose.

———

But then came a summer when the rain kept falling . . . and falling and falling. It fell with a fury I had rarely seen, and it kept coming, one violent drop after another, one day after another.

The ground became saturated, and with every hour of rainfall, the river deepened; then it widened, and when it became clear that the river's banks could hold no more water, one more storm rolled onto the horizon.

I'll never forget seeing the river gush over its walls and out into the town. It was fierce, washing away bridges and barns, doing damage that would shake this community for months, if not years. Crops were washed away, a brand-new hotel was flooded, and people were hurt—*really* hurt—because of that little river. Cars were trapped half-submerged on roadways, police piloted little boats on drenched farmland in hopes of rescuing trapped inhabitants, and another memorable chapter in local history—and round of unbelievable stories—was created again. The culture was tattooed with another moment when the river changed everything. Tears flowed over family dinners, worry raged, and destinies changed. The friendly pussycat had erupted into a roaring lion and left mere rubble in her wake.

I learned that day that a flood is uncontrollable; it goes where it likes and does what it wants, and even the smallest streams can became cataclysmic forces of nature.

IN JESUS, GRACE BROKE ITS BANK

In a less devastating sense, that flood in that little town reminds me of the force with which grace soaked the earth with the arrival of Jesus. Grace didn't flow like a trickling stream, barely leaking from beneath the snowpack on a tall mountain. It wasn't a polite little brook minding its own business as it curved around mountains. Grace flowed from heaven like water gushing from a breached dam.

The arrival of grace was a tsunami that changed eternity, reshaped religion, and redefined everything—forever.

When the prophet Isaiah described the arrival of the Messiah, I think he must have been remembering a flood he had himself witnessed. In the wake of the flood of grace on a barren, broken earth, Isaiah imagined a moment when

> the eyes of the blind [will] be opened and the ears of the deaf unstopped. Then will the lame leap like a deer, and the mute tongue shout for joy. Water will gush forth in the wilderness and streams in the desert. The burning sand will become a pool, the thirsty ground bubbling springs. In the haunts where jackals once lay, grass and reeds and papyrus will grow. . . . Those the LORD has rescued will return. They will enter Zion with singing; everlasting joy will crown their heads. Gladness and joy will overtake them. (Isa. 35:5–7, 10)

Jesus' redeeming death and resurrection unleashed a torrent of undeserved love and grace. It has been saturating the globe ever since its advent. It has become the great ideal of literature, the transcendent motif of the arts, and the design of redemption that has influenced all facets of society and culture. It's from this great epic that every heroic tale of life and love, of war and peace, and of courage and cowardice has drawn the core of its story. This great idea of redemption that weaves its way through popular culture and literature was God's idea from the very first. It's no wonder that every time we watch a movie or read a book or hear a story that embraces this great, transcendent story, we feel as if we're listening to a chord struck in our own hearts.

Our hearts were tuned to play in harmony with God. Jesus'

death was the missing note to make the harmony happen, and grace the hammer that struck it. Now our relationship with him can play in sweet harmony as grace continues to make the music possible.

It's because we are listening to a chord struck within our own hearts that Jesus seems so important to us when we first hear of his story. It's the story of God speaking to us in our birth language, addressing the problems we know we have but don't know how to define. Grace is the key that unlocks something that has long been locked within us.

It's as if God is speaking to us—because, in fact, he *is* speaking to us.

And he didn't speak in a whisper at the cross. He roared at us. He screamed at the top of his lungs that he loved us. He pierced the night with his bellowing cry, *"I LOVE YOU!"*

Satan is defeated. Man is forgiven. Everything has changed.

Really. Everything.

God didn't come to our dry, grace-starved hearts like a gardener with a little bucket to trickle some water on us. No, God turned an irrigation hose of grace onto our dry souls and drenched us. He drenched us so thoroughly that his living water reached the very roots of our beings, and it was so strong it almost ripped them from their roots.

His love was fierce, overwhelming, destiny defining. And in that moment when God floods our souls, everything changes, *forever.*

A TORRENT OF LOVE

The God who is pulling and twisting the levers of history is also *our* designer. He knows what to say to activate what he's hidden in our hearts, and in grace he speaks to our spiritual neglect and frustration; he speaks to the part of us that doesn't feel good enough and the part of us that feels as if God is angry with us.

When Andrea, my wife, speaks to me, she speaks differently from anyone else in the world because she knows me in a way that no one else does. She knows everything about me, the good and the bad, and she knows what I'm thinking even when I'm not expressing it. She knows how I actually feel even when I carefully bury those feelings under layers and layers of façade.

I can't lie to her, I can't deceive her, I can't be someone I'm not to her, and I can't hide anything from her. It's simply impossible. We're so close that she can almost read my mind. In fact, sometimes I think she *can* read my mind.

Yet somehow, despite my many flaws and weaknesses and my aptitude to repeat mistakes I should have long overcome, she still loves me.

All the more, Jesus has loved us and given us grace that would even forgive Hitler and Bin Laden and Pol Pot and Genghis Khan if they would have just repented and accepted it. Jesus' love and Jesus' grace are so great it's scandalous—too much to bear, and too easy to get, and that's why it's always been so controversial.

That's also why it's so remarkable.

Grace accepts us as we are but is too powerful and too transformative to leave us as we are. Despite everything God knows about us, and despite the ten thousand different ways that we've allowed ourselves to become separated from him, he has chosen to love us, and he has chosen *grace* rather than the punishment we deserve.

God didn't cautiously divvy out grace to the deserving. He

broke the dam, and let it rush loosely and wildly into history. Jesus grabbed us by the nape of the neck and thrust us into its drenching, transformative flow.

We are clean, and I can hear God's bellowing laughter of joy at the sight of it all.

EIGHT

—

CHRISTIANS SHOULD BE
HAPPY, FOR GOD'S SAKE

OKAY, I MAY RANT A LITTLE HERE.

I believe grace should make us happy, but some of us aren't easily made happy.

Maybe you're like me. I grew up in a hyperconservative culture, and conservatives aren't exactly known for being the life of the party.

My family wasn't just conservative. We dwelled somewhere to the right of Attila the Hun. To us "the liberals" weren't just proponents of certain policies; they were mysterious, probably communist, infiltrators of America, bent upon hijacking the nation and handing it on a silver platter to Chairman Mao.

In rural South Carolina, I'm not even sure I ever knew a *liberal*. I had heard of them, but I didn't know one. This species of human was as onerous and mystifying to us as Sasquatch or the Loch Ness Monster. *Liberal* was roughly synonymous with *demon possessed*.

We were so conservative that I'm pretty sure some folks in my family were concerned that my willingness to share my toys in kindergarten might have been a first, dangerous step toward socialism. I mean, Welch's grape juice was a little *too close* to wine for us, and we were also convinced that America was already on the verge of the Apocalypse until, in one magnificent example of the grace of God, he sent us a prophet called the Fox News Channel. From that day forward, we had the Fox News Channel playing on every television in the house nearly every waking moment of the day. One time, I even wrote an essay to defend a conservative commentator because someone said he wasn't a Christian, and I couldn't imagine that there was a difference between a conservative and a Christian.

Some people I knew were so conservative that they even believed rock music was filled with subliminal satanic messages, and that America's first step down the slippery slope to hell was when Elvis Presley started gyrating those hips of his. I'm sure we didn't know the difference between John Lennon and Lenin.

Our conservatism was no more potent than in our religion. We specialized in truth, but grace—sort of—escaped us.

We were Baptists with a capital, boldface *B*—we carried big old KJV study Bibles to Sunday school classes by the time we were in fourth grade, and we were taught that our faith was a deathly serious matter. We were "saved by grace," *of course*, but we were also always walking on the thin tightrope over an abyss of "worldliness" that couldn't any longer send us to hell but could, sure as hell, make our lives miserable. Christianity was supposed to be the best thing in life, but to me it seemed suspicious. When the preacher would be yelling at the top of his lungs, with veins sticking out on his forehead, about how "happy" he was being a Christian, I felt as if I were watching one of those infomercials where a guy with too much hair spray is trying to convince me that I can buy a miracle in a bottle for ten bucks. Usually those folks, too, try to persuade me that "this'll change your life."

I never had any money to buy the stuff the guy on TV was peddling, but it always disappointed me when I heard people say that they had and it didn't work like he'd said it would.

It seemed to me that the yelling preachers weren't just trying to convince their parishioners that Jesus would *change their lives.* It felt as if they were trying to convince themselves. Yelling at people to be happy was just off-putting to me. And ironic—like when Michael Moore rails against capitalism one fifty-thousand dollar speech at a time.

There I go—being a conservative again!

Frankly, it's no wonder to me that plenty of skeptical people don't want a thing to do with Christianity. I've met my share of Christians whose facial expressions alone make them look as though they've downed a steady diet of lemons and raw eggs. More so, our self-righteousness, and our disconnection from people whose worlds are unlike ours, sometimes makes others see an inauthentic Christianity that isn't filled with joy and love and grace and delight, but rather with duty and obligation and disappointment and self-deception.

Christians might be thought of as holy, but they're not always thought of as very happy.

Is this okay? Does Jesus want us *happy* or *holy*?

In a letter to the American author Sheldon Vanauken, C. S. Lewis once wrote, "It is a Christian duty, as you know, for everyone to be as happy as he can."[1]

Was he right?

I think so. God's grace ought to make us happy people, period.

THE LADY WE WERE SCARED OF

Yet sometimes the most religious people seem to live the most undesirable lives.

Take, for instance, this lady at my church when I was a kid. She would have disagreed with C. S. Lewis, for sure. She didn't appear to believe that happiness and holiness could possibly coexist.

Christianity was solemn business, and she had this unsmiling "righteousness" about her that caused all of us to shake in our boots at the very mention of her name. We knew that she was not just *committed* to lecturing us delinquents when we strayed down the wide road to destruction—she *enjoyed* it. She was intimidating, and that intimidating aura was her pride and joy. She introduced people to a Jesus who was always looking over your shoulder, awaiting his next opportunity to clobber you across the head if you even thought of doing something *bad*. Jesus was tough, aloof, and angry.

Like the yelling preacher, she would teach "that God so *loved* the world . . ." but this was a different kind of love than the love I had heard about. This wasn't a love *better than* the love of the "world"—it was less: more judgmental, condemning, and soaked in guilt. There wasn't a lot of grace in this love that she was preaching about. She gave lots of lip service to "grace," but it wasn't believable.

Somehow, this rough-and-tumble, graceless view of "Jesus the judge" got ingrained in me, and its roots run so deep in my heart that it has taken an enormous amount of effort to actually believe what I know to be true about the grace of Jesus. I've often said that one of the most profound truths I've ever learned is that

Jesus isn't mad at me. He actually cares for me, and he's looking out for me. Even when Jesus is disciplining me or convicting me or trying to change me, his motivation is from a place of kindness and gentleness and love. It is grace that compels his most prophetic sermons. He actually wants my life to be better, to be happier, and to feel more fulfilling.

What has been even more difficult is trying to see Jesus as an actual person who walked on earth. It has been hard for me to imagine Jesus sitting with children and eating breakfast with his mother and chilling out with his disciples, sharing inside jokes and laughing until he almost couldn't breathe. It's interesting how my immature view of the grace of God also inhibited me from seeing the humanity of Jesus. I never imagined that Jesus laughed, for instance. I read the Scriptures with an almost singular filter of *Jesus the judge.* Now, as you can tell by reading this book, I've begun to see so much more of Jesus through the lens of grace.

Grace helps me even see the sarcasm of Jesus, like when he looked at the Pharisees and said, in Luke 15:7, "There will be more joy in heaven over one sinner who repents than over ninety-nine just persons who *need no repentance*" (NKJV, emphasis added), or in Matthew when he mocked the Pharisees' concern about straining gnats out of their soup while simultaneously swallowing a whole camel in their hypocrisy. In the biblical language, there's a pun in the text. Jesus said, "You're so concerned about a *galma*, but you're eating *gamla* every day!"

I can see the crowd saying, "Snap!"

Jesus told the Pharisees that they should really stop looking at specks in other people's eyes when they have logs protruding out of their own. This was funny stuff. Grace has helped me see Jesus' humanity, and seeing his humanity helps me believe that he also understands me.

Can't you see Jesus smiling when he heard the crowd laugh at the Pharisees?

You should. Jesus smiled, believe it or not.

Jesus was no curmudgeon. He laughed and joked and had a good time. He snickered and playfully picked on people and intentionally turned a phrase to rouse a crowd.

He had a sense of humor because he was a human giving grace to humans. Jesus knew what it was like to stub your toe and to get food stuck in your teeth and to have a crick in your neck and to really, really want to be someone different sometimes. He knew how to laugh with that kind of gut laugh where you're so tickled you almost can't contain yourself, you cackle till you can't breathe, and then just when you get your composure, another wave hits the shore.

THE BIBLE SAYS JESUS BROUGHT JOY

Remember, it was shepherds who were the recipients of the press release announcing Jesus' arrival. They were tending their sheep at night, as they did every night, and then suddenly the stillness of the night was shattered by the sound of music. The shepherds freaked out (as you would!).

Just as the shepherds thought that aliens from Mars had finally decided to do away with Earth, an angel said, "Do not be afraid. I bring you good news that will cause great joy for all the people."[2]

Isn't that interesting?

There are thousands of words that they could have chosen and those thousands of words could have been organized in a million different ways, and yet the angel decided the most appropriate words to describe the greatest moment in history were these words: "I bring you *good news* that will *cause great joy* for all people."

The arrival of Jesus was *good news* and *great joy*.

In the original language, this verse is actually redundant. The word for *good news* (which is sometimes translated as "gospel") is actually the combination of the Greek words for "news" and "joyful." The author is, in a sense, saying, "I bring you *joyful news* that will cause *great joy* for *all* people!"

Why?

It's simple. The injection of joy into humanity is a primary implication of the arrival of Jesus into our lives. Tim Keller elaborated on this even further when he wrote of the historical applications of this phrase *good news* in *King's Cross*:

> There is an ancient Roman inscription from about the same time as Jesus. . . . It starts: "The beginning of the gospel of Caesar Augustus." It's the story of the birth and coronation of the Roman emperor. A gospel was news of some event that changed things in a meaningful way. It could be an ascension to the throne, or it could be a victory. When Greece was invaded by Persia and the Greeks won the great battles of Marathon and Solnus, they sent heralds (or evangelists) who proclaimed the good news to the cities: "We have fought for you, we have won, and now you're no longer slaves; you're free." A gospel is an announcement of something that has happened in history, something that's been done for you that changes your status forever.[3]

I'm not sure that the legalism of my overly conservative roots, or the heavy-handedness of that Sunday school teacher who caused shivers to run up our spines, reflects the kind of *joy* and *good news* that is at the core of Jesus' arrival and redemption of planet Earth. Grace kills guilt with *joy*.

The gospel is *good news* about life and not *bad news* about how disappointed I should be with myself and the grueling experience it is to be a Christian.

Jesus endured a grueling experience so that we wouldn't have to.

That's good news—great news, in fact!

Jesus arrived with the intent of totally turning the religious system on its head, and his weapon against that system's hypocrisy and legalism was *grace*. When we keep grace at an arm's length, religion will always deconstruct into *duty* motivated by *obligation*. Even worse, we'll drain the fun out of our faith.

Jesus believed that God's kindness was motivational enough to keep God's children on the straight and narrow, and that he could relieve the pressure of the fear of judgment without jeopardizing the holiness of his people.

Their pursuit of holiness could be a celebration—a joyous celebration of God's relentless grace, rather than a long and arduous walk up a mountain of righteousness that you know you'll never summit.

Jesus unseated the self-righteous and put the forgiven in their place. He pried open the long-locked prison doors of legalism to let the light of the grace of God flood that dark and difficult cellar, and then he dared to tell us that with his grace comes his joy. It's a two-for-one deal.

DOES JESUS WANT US TO
BE HAPPY OR HOLY?

So does Jesus want us to be happy or holy? The answer is *yes!*

He helps us live a life of holiness *and* happiness, and that is the *good news*. Jesus' efforts to redeem us didn't simply establish another religion. They were the announcement of a totally new thing. A new king was now on the throne, and he was sharing his wealth with the populace and making a new life possible for everyone!

Even when Jesus was scolding his disciples about the necessity of keeping the commands he had given them, his next sentence provided a different kind of promise and motivation: "I have told you this so that my *joy* may be in you and that your *joy* may be complete."[4] And don't forget that Jesus' most famous sermon begins with the Beatitudes. Those little dictums of counterintuitive advice begin with the word *blessed*—a word that is sometimes translated as *happy*. Jesus is saying, "Do you want to be happy? Then do these things."

That's the point, by the way: Jesus' grace not only gives us a ticket to heaven. He has also given us joy.

But it's also important to understand what *happiness* actually means. It's a word that has often been minimized until it simply means having enough money in the bank and the right car in the driveway or the right kind of house in the right kind of neighborhood.

This isn't happiness. This is materialism. It's a temporary substitute for happiness. There are lots of other substitutes too, and one of the reasons we don't think we'll ever be happy is because we've never, or at least rarely, experienced the real thing. C. S. Lewis spoke famously of the unfortunate contentment we have with the generic when *real* happiness is available to us.

> Indeed, if we consider the unblushing promises of reward and the staggering nature of the rewards promised in the Gospels, it would seem that Our Lord finds our desires not too strong, but too weak. We are half-hearted creatures, fooling about with drink and sex and ambition when infinite joy is offered us, like an ignorant child who wants to go on making mud pies in a slum because he cannot imagine what is meant by an offer of a holiday at the sea. We are far too easily pleased.[5]

In Jesus' time happiness meant the virtue of having *joy and satisfaction with your place in life.*[6]

Some philosophers believed that the achievement of happiness in a person's or city's or country's life was the ultimate goal, or the ultimate virtue. Achieving this happiness would make you feel complete and satisfied. It would help you find, and realize, all the possible joy in your place in life.

SEEING OUR FAITH THROUGH THE LENS OF JOY

We have a reason to be joyful.

Think of your spiritual life as spring-cleaning. If I have to clean alone, I have a tendency to grunt and complain my way room to room as I crawl and scrub and clean and pry the long-settled dust out of the corners and crevices.

If my wife and I make an adventure out of it, or if I start cleaning with music or a podcast in my ears, my attitude automatically shifts.

Better yet, I sometimes stop to remember the day we arrived in our town house after our honeymoon. We had boxes of wedding gifts piled to the ceiling. We had dishes to wash and items to return and a ton of work to do, but there was a sense of celebration about that moment. It just didn't feel like work because it was all wrapped in such a beautiful moment of life. We were just married, and everything was infused with joy.

Isn't it interesting that Jesus often used the analogy of marriage to describe our new relationship with God that began with our salvation? When we begin to appreciate grace, the same sense of joy ought to infuse everything we do. Jesus told his disciples that an appropriate response as we understand our new lifestyle in Christ is to "rejoice in that day and leap for joy" (Luke 6:23).

When you start to look at your faith through the lens of joy, things change for the good. Faith is no longer the death of your old self (and your old fun and old freedom and old life). Faith is the injection of *real* life into what you *thought* was life.

The mentality you have about your relationship with Jesus is just as important as walking in the truth, because the lens through which you view things changes everything. Your attitude makes it easier to, as I've written in *Honestly*, "live what you say you believe."[7] Perception is enormously powerful.

The story of Alfred Nobel is a showstopping illustration of the power of perception.

Nobel was the scientist who conceived and created dynamite.

It was in April 1888, just after his brother Ludvig had died, that he was flipping nonchalantly through his favorite French newspaper in his laboratory and turned to the obituary section to read of his brother's passing. He was horrified to discover that the paper had mistakenly recorded that it was *Alfred* who had died, and not his brother Ludvig. Alfred sat there fully alive, reading his own obituary. As the inventor of dynamite, he was characterized as a "merchant of death" whose personal fortune had come from his discovery of "a new way to mutilate and kill."

Nobel was shocked. The obituary took him into the future, allowing him to view his eventual legacy through the words of this mistaken reporter. It was more than surreal, and this singular experience prompted him to almost immediately designate his fortune to the establishment of annual "Nobel Prizes" in physics, chemistry, medicine, literature, and peace. These prizes, for which he is now most famous, would be conferred upon those who had in the preceding year made the greatest contribution to the benefit of mankind.[8]

This simple shift in perspective, from death to life, has had repercussions for the good of mankind for more than a century.

This is the power of perspective. And perhaps the same power will be activated in our own relationships with Jesus when we start to look at our faith through the lens of joy, realizing the generosity of God's grace.

It should cause us to leap with joy at the very thought of Jesus.

NINE

HOW TO MISS THE GRACE OF GOD

THE GLASS WAS A FAMILY HEIRLOOM, PASSED from generation to generation.

It lived on the corner of the highest shelf in the room, placed there because of its delicacy. There, it was beyond the reach of the children, high enough to avoid the ruckus of a busy family room, and still within sight of everyone who might come by and admire its beauty.

Eventually, it was forgotten. Day after day of neglect caused the slow shifting of the house to nudge the glass toward the edge of the shelf—until it was teetering perilously.

One last jog through the living room decided its fate. The glass fell with a great crash, and shattered into a thousand pieces.

So goes the fate of even the most cherished thing when inattention causes one to forget how valuable, and fragile, a treasure it is.

Grace is God's most priceless gift, but your wonderment

won't keep you from replacing it, eventually, with mere religion. Faith is a fragile thing, and it's easier to fake than flourish.

If you don't live out grace in your everyday life, your faith will end up on a respirator. How does one train oneself to live it out?

WHAT HAPPENS WHEN YOU FAKE IT

Faking it always causes problems.

Literally *everyone* on planet Earth received a potent shot of surprise in 2008 as the world's citizens watched the unraveling of her economies. From the impoverished widow in sub-Saharan Africa who saw an impossible increase in the price of the food she needed to feed her five children, to the Fortune 500 CEO who watched his financial house teeter and fall in the aftershock of the collapse of the markets, everyone felt as if something in the world had broken. Some kind of levee had been breached, and now people everywhere were looking for whatever they could find to throw into the hole before the rush of water drowned them and everyone with them.

Something that no one expected had happened, and it caused presidents and prime ministers to sweat as though they were taking a test they hadn't studied for. It even stumped the greatest financial minds of our times. The people the rest of us expected to be able to solve these sorts of things from their ivory towers were downing their gin out of golden goblets and scratching their heads in confusion and disbelief. It was as if an earthquake had happened, but this earthquake wasn't content to rumble for five or ten or twenty-five seconds. This quaking wouldn't let up until it had shaken to its foundation every institution that thought it couldn't fail. The Dow took a nosedive, banks failed and had to be artificially propped up at taxpayers' expense, and many of the world's rich and powerful leaders found themselves manhandled by something too big for even them. After all, it was their debt too, and they were as worried as the rest of us.

We thought they had it under control, and they wished they did.

History has a way of doing this to us just when everyone seems drunk on his or her success. Banks were approving loans that they must have known the people receiving the money couldn't afford, and nearly all of us, if only in our unconscious minds, thought of money as something we were entitled to more than something we had to work for and protect.

History turned another corner and reminded us that our money is not a source of security, and this time the assumption that America would always fly above the unpredictable volatility of the world's financial markets went the way of Pompeii and Atlantis. America's stabilizing force within the world's sometimes-unpredictable markets had been replaced with a reality that America could also *take down the world with us*. It remains, in some ways, as if a new chapter in history is unfolding as nations like China and Brazil rise in their influence while America still stumbles through its own maze—perhaps almost to the exit, but still a little drunk on her own power. Lincoln's adage is worth remembering: "Nearly all men can stand adversity, but if you want to test a man's character, give him power."[1]

Decades from now, my students will learn that two distinct events marked the beginning of the Great Recession. One was more technical and of economic significance and the other was of more popular concern, but it was the mix of the two that injected the anxiety that caused the beginning and especially the perpetuation

of the financial crisis. The first was when the fourth-largest investment bank in the nation, Lehman Brothers, failed. Every investor
and every economist in the country felt electricity run down their
spines as they watched a bastion of the American economy
make her shocking crash. The fall of Lehman Brothers was—to
many—as unlikely as the crash of the World Trade Centers on
September 11, 2001. Within the same decade, these two unlikely
events brought a one-two punch to the gut in a city that is the
barometer of the world's economy. Second, from a more popular
perspective, the indiscretions of a famous investor whose name—
Bernard Madoff—will give generations an easy way to remember
his historical significance. He *made off* with billions as he operated
history's most complex, and successful, Ponzi scheme.

Both Lehman Brothers and Madoff had one characteristic
in common, and it's the same characteristic that was shared by
the long-forgotten precursors to the Great Recession, Enron and
WorldCom.

They acted as if they were something they were not, and they
became so adept at having just enough in order to look the part
that eventually they seemed to have forgotten that they were more
like paper tigers. Whether it was Madoff defrauding people of billions or Lehman Brothers taking on excessive risk by gambling
on the once-lucrative subprime mortgage market, each looked
like a successful financier.

In actuality, their financial activities were not a true indication that they were stable, successful, and operating with integrity
and profit. Because, in truth, they were none of those things.

Their "works" were "dead." Or at least dying.

The whole scenario isn't that dissimilar from our own propensity to practice *religion* without actually having a *relationship*

with God. The whole slew of spiritual activities that we engage in can actually be as substanceless as the transactions passing through a bank that's sinking fast.

Either way, it's the same vice. *Looking good* isn't the same as *being good*. Faking it never works.

Receiving the grace of God, through Jesus, might welcome us into the kingdom of God, it might forgive our sins, it might even make us "new creations," but it doesn't mean that we're free of the temptation of faking it.

It becomes easy to act religious, going through all the motions, without really enjoying the relationship with God that grace has granted, or taking advantage of the opportunity we have to give that grace to others.

Here's a line that has become a cliché for the good reason that it's an obvious truth: lots of people are religious, but there's a difference between religion and a relationship with God.

AN ATHENIAN PROBLEM

When Paul arrived in Athens after being run out of town in Berea, he went right to the place called Areopagus, the cultural, religious, philosophical heart of the great city of intellectuals. Athens was the city whose constitution was argued and recorded by Aristotle's students, and from the ingenuity of its elite came institution after institution and idea after idea that in some sense still undergird much of our modern society. Chances were, during Paul's time, that if you were the best in the world at anything, you had roots in Athens. Since Paul spent much of his time traveling to the seats of power around the world, eventually he made it here too.

The hill known as Areopagus was just down from the Acropolis. It was where the intellectual elite spent their days in argument and debate about the latest ideas being popularized in Greco-Roman society. The philosophers, whose job, literally, was to discuss things all day, mainly fit within two categories. There were the Epicureans, who believed that everything happened by chance and that death was the end of everything. They believed that the gods were remote from the world and did not care, and that pleasure was the chief purpose in life. The Epicureans could be the love children of our modern deists and hedonists.

The other group was the Stoics. They believed that everything that happened was the will of God and therefore must be accepted without resentment, and that every so often, the world disintegrated and was burnt up and started all over again on the same cycle of events.[2] The Stoics could be the children of our modern pantheists and fatalists.

Interestingly, when you read the account of Paul's preaching there in the Areopagus, you find that he was incredibly well versed in their own ideas about the world. He quoted their poets and spoke a polemic filled with innuendos that would unlock certain things in their informed, philosophical minds.

Listening to Paul speak with the Stoics and Epicureans there was like listening to the science nerds in your eleventh-grade physics class talking with numbers as if they were words. You would stand there listening to what was a kind of foreign language only mastered by the kind of people who mix chemicals for fun and use magnifying glasses to look at insects and keep their lucky pens in their pocket protectors and carry bags of books.

Paul wasn't speaking from the outside in. He was speaking from the inside out. It seems as he if understood them so well that he was able to speak as one of them, and the introduction to his speech reveals what the primary issue was that separated them from knowing God as he should be known. They were deeply religious, among the most knowledgeable people in the modern world, yet somehow they were strangely separated from God.

Paul walked in the court and began to speak with these words:

> Men of Athens, I see that you're very religious. As I was passing through, considering the objects of your worship, I even found an altar to an unknown god. This God, whom you worship without knowing, I proclaim to you. (Acts 17:22–23)

Now, you probably read those words too quickly. Read them again, slowly, carefully.

> *Men of Athens* [the most intelligent and educated in the world], *I see that you're very religious* [they were involved in all kinds of spiritual practices]. *As I was passing through* [which implies that this place was so religious, there was evidence of their religiosity everywhere], *considering the objects of your worship* [then he got curious and started looking more closely], *I even found an altar to an unknown god* [Paul discovered a "just in case" altar]. *This God, whom you worship without knowing, I proclaim to you* [he will use this as his hook to connect them to the gospel].

Athens was dripping with religion. It was a city "of many gods." In fact, "it was said that there were more statues of the gods in Athens than in all the rest of Greece put together, and that in Athens it was easier to meet a god than another person."[3]

If you could measure people's spiritual health by the amount of religious activity they were engaged in, then Athens must have been the healthiest city in the entire world. But Paul knew, coming himself from a very religious background as a Jewish scholar par excellence, that *religious activity* implied nothing about one's *relationship* with God.

Our religious activity is no indication whatsoever as to whether we actually know God or not. In fact, in some cases, the zealousness and quantity of one's religious activity may be a pretty good indication that he does not know God at all, but wants the rest of us, and probably God as well, to think he does.

Paul said to Athenians, as he could say to many modern, religious people who attend church every Sunday, "You're worshipping a god that you don't even know! This is absurd!"

Paul was speaking to "pagans" in a city filled with idol worship, yet it seems that many of us who profess faith in Jesus Christ are inflicted with the same spiritual problem. We're worshipping a God that we don't *know*, and we're pros at *looking good, looking religious*, but having very little actual *commitment to* or *understanding of* our faith.

We're recipients of grace, members of the family and kingdom of God, but we never take it any farther than that. We don't live in response to that grace, and we don't treat others with the same grace with which Christ has treated us.

"LOOKING RELIGIOUS" IS NEVER ENOUGH

It's very clear that what Paul found as a problem for *pagans* was also a problem for those who were most educated in what existed of the Scriptures in Jesus' day. The Pharisees, who had at least the first five books of the Bible memorized, were just as much victims of the disease of just being *religious*. They were just as guilty of filling their lives with spiritual activity without actually *knowing* God. There was less of a difference between the Greek philosophers and the Pharisees than you may think.

This should especially worry those of us who are inclined toward religious or "spiritual" interests.

It's clear from the lives of the Pharisees that we can know our theology, memorize our Bibles, live every commandment perfectly, and yet somehow miss the essential truth that we're *working* for.

We can be involved in all kinds of religious activity without actually *knowing* God. How does this happen?

It's that word *work* that's the problem. The Pharisees thought they could work hard enough to impress God enough to persuade him to grant them his grace and favor. The more they worked, visibly and publicly, the better they looked on the outside, but somehow they never let God get to the inside. So they became proud—hypocritical and judgmental and condemning. The very ones who should have been most prepared to sight the Messiah became the ones most dedicated to getting rid of him.

Why did the teachers who had memorized large portions of the Bible and who lived their lives for the arrival of the Messiah totally miss it?

It's actually simple. They measured their proximity to God by the sum of their spiritual activities. Their church attendance, Bible reading, deep spiritual discussions, and total number of admirers and disciples, all convinced them that they were good enough.

Eventually, you start to believe you don't need God—that

grace is for other people, people who are less holy and not as religious as you. You have your life together.

So there they were, caught in a whirlwind of spiritual activity, ignorant of their need to know God and to depend upon him above all other things, and deluded especially about their ability to work their way into heaven on their own merits. They had become more impressed with themselves than they were with God—and far more impressed with themselves than God was with them.

This eventually soured into an arrogance and self-deception that blinded them more and more to their need for God. Sure, they talked a good game, sounding as if they needed him—but they lived as though they didn't. They taught that a man's spiritual health was contingent upon the grace of God, but they were measuring their own spiritual health by how much better they were than everyone else.

Arrogance and self-deception, not grace and mercy, are the products of *being religious* without nurturing a relationship with God. We begin to act as if we're miniature gods, we get a false sense of self-importance, and we deny ourselves the opportunity to know the grace of the real Jesus, whom we can actually *know* as we *know a friend.*

IT'S JUST EVERYWHERE

The elevation of "looking" over actually "being" is ever present in our modern world. Looking good is enough as long as you can maintain the public deception, or, worse yet, as long as you can keep deceiving yourself.

This is nowhere more evident than in our culture's secular religion of politics. I call it a "religion" because each campaign has its own doctrines and prescribed behaviors and godlike figure. People follow this figure and his or her agenda almost blindly and often sacrificially—giving their time, talent, and treasure to ensure that, when a campaign season is done, their idol has received the most worship possible.

What's worse is that now we have career politicians who consider it their vocation. America's founders never imagined that professional, career politicians would run our nation. They imagined a nation that would be steered in the right direction by citizen legislators who would set their *real* careers aside for a time, when elected by their community, to serve the greater good of the nation. So they would temporarily go to Washington, DC, to serve their communities (not themselves!).

Today, politics has devolved into some kind of complex public relations career focused almost entirely on self-service and self-worship. Politicians work really hard at one thing: *looking good.* They pay a lot of money to a lot of advisers and make a lot of decisions just to accomplish that one goal. The problem is, *looking good* isn't the same as *being good.* It's no longer about the good of the people the politicians represent; it's about their electability in future elections, and about their own image. Certain people just *look electable.* Others win support because of how much money they have or who they know. Politicians are often bloviating public relations guys talking with supreme conviction on matters they know nothing about.

We love to mock and dismiss politicians as despicable and self-serving, but the truth is that we all, to a greater or lesser degree, do the same thing—especially when it comes to our religion.

Like me, as a kid you were probably a quick study in the importance of *looking the part*. Within weeks of entering school, you started learning that if you wore the right clothes you would be popular, or if you acted the right way you would be cool, or if you said and did certain things you would be worthy of acceptance. The first time I remember being overcome by this pressure was at the end of my sixth-grade year. My teacher would ask each of her students to fill out a one-page profile at the end of the school year so she could remember them.

One of the questions was, "What is your favorite band?"

I can still remember staring blankly at that question for a long time in a moral dilemma. I wasn't cool. I had never been cool. I was a repellent to cool. But I knew that this one-page description of me would live on forever. I knew there was nothing interesting about me, but I didn't want generations of sixth graders after me to know that. So I sat staring at that piece of paper and contemplated committing my first public lie on that piece of paper, just in an effort to *look good*.

Despite the fact that I, even as a sixth grader, had singlehandedly started, written, published, edited, and sold our school's first newspaper, and despite making enough money on the project to fund weeks of field trips for my class, I had somehow remained uncool and unpopular. I decided that this was my chance to restore my reputation. I decided to lie.

To this day, you can probably climb into the archives of that rural elementary school and find scribbled on that piece of paper the name of a band that everyone else liked. I had none of their albums and had hardly heard their songs (and I didn't even like them), but I had been trained to be someone I wasn't if it would make me admired, envied, accepted, or respected by my peers. The next best thing to being something is to fake it.

And you probably think I'm making a big deal out of nothing, right? Over-spiritualizing a child's bout with peer pressure, and exaggerating the scope of this internal war we all face?

Actually, I'm not exaggerating. In fact, I'm doing the exact opposite: I'm actually lessening the significance of the enormous damage this particular social vice has done to the body of Christ in our modern times. Precisely because we think of it as the common cold, we've failed to realize that it is a bleeding ulcer, poisoning us from the inside.

It has caused *hypocrisy* to run amok, and it has gravely damaged the church by making us display an unlived faith to a world searching for *real faith*. It has also led us to create a Christian façade with no substance behind it. We're deceiving not only everyone else but also ourselves—and we aren't even aware of it.

We've learned that living a fake life can pay major dividends if we can do it well enough for long enough. We begin to believe that it's almost as good to just *act like it* as it is to *be* it.

It has become far more important to look like you should than it is to be who you should be. Professing Christians are taught to be like display homes with carefully manicured lawns in gorgeous neighborhoods, but despite their perfect exteriors, there's nothing inside and nobody home.

In fact, it's even worse. The house that looks perfect from the outside, and even enviable to those riding by, is more than empty. It's actually rotting from the inside out. The house that looks so good isn't even livable. It looks as it should, but it's not actually a house. It's a shell, like a Hollywood set, and the longer we substitute spiritual activity for spiritual depth, the more we become merely a shell of who we might have been.

It's just one big Ponzi scheme.

The first step to getting grace, and the first step to giving it to a world that desperately needs it, is to be honest with yourself about your own relationship with God.

The liberating truth of Christianity is that God's grace means you don't have to try so hard. He meets you halfway, takes you as you are, and loves you too much to leave you there.

He specializes in welcoming people into his kingdom despite their flaws, foibles, and imperfections.

You can stop the masquerade. Jesus knew what he was getting himself into.

PART 2

GIVING GRACE

TEN

WHAT'S GOOD ABOUT DEATH

THE SWEAT WAS STILL BEADING ON MY FORE-
head when it actually sank in.

I had almost died.

We had just completed nine full hours of hiking up a serpen-
tine path to the summit of two fourteen-thousand-foot cliffs in
Colorado. I could barely stand, let alone think, but one thing was
clear. A delicate twist of fate could have made that afternoon my
last. The last for all four of us, in fact. Instead, we were trying to
find enough oxygen to catch our breath again.

For sure, I was a little more shaken than the others. They were
old hands at this rugged adventure stuff. They climbed rocks with,
and without, ropes. They mountain-biked rocky trails that clung
to the edge of mountains overlooking deep, dangerous precipices.
They were the kinds of people who looked with the same awe at
the survivalist skills of Bear Grylls that I reserve for C. S. Lewis,
Churchill, Dickens, and Lincoln. They would eat bugs *just 'cause*
and get a good burst of adrenaline when their nice spring hike was
interrupted by a lightning storm and torrential rain.

Once, I was hiking with them up an unmarked trail because

we saw a crag from the road that we (meaning they) wanted to climb. Everything was moving along quite nicely until our hike down. Within minutes we were lost, roaming aimlessly through deeper and deeper forest without any clue which direction we were going. The sun was slowly setting, darkening the already imposing shadows of the towering trees around us, and in the distance, I could hear the rustle of those animals that only go bump in the night. My nerves were already on edge when we stumbled upon the ramshackle house owned by the local mountain man. He had the kind of beard you'd expect; he was shirtless, with a machete in his right hand and a gleam in his eye. The kind of gleam you see moments before your final breath in one of those scary movies.

The mountain man warned us about "coming this way again," and he didn't flinch when he told us, "This is how people like you get shot in the woods, and if you ever come back on my property, I might have to shoot you myself."

I didn't sleep for a week.

They thought this was cool.

I thought this was dangerous.

It's amazing that we were all best friends, and it's even more amazing that they had somehow persuaded me to fly all the way to Colorado to climb two fourteen-thousand-foot mountains. I must have temporarily lost my mind.

As you've probably deduced by now, I'm not exactly the mountain-climbing type. I'm short. If I have muscles, I've never found them, and I'm just not an outdoorsy person.

Just last night I opened the bathroom window while scrubbing the bathtub. A scary little insect of some sort that looked like the love child of a wasp and a spider flew through the barely cracked window and landed within a few inches of my right hand. I jolted backward in sheer terror as if some great puppet master had pulled my string a little too hard.

For the next ten minutes, I engaged in a fateful dance with that little ogre. Like some ancient story unfolding in slow motion, first we sized each other up. Then the ogre struck first, and barely missed me. I stepped back to regroup, caught my breath, and then dove in again. I hit him, but I wasn't strong enough to kill him. He struck back and missed. Then I hit him again.

He wasn't fazed.

And I didn't have a grenade.

So, in a fit of medieval courage, I sidestepped the ogre and slammed the bathroom door, locking the two of us inside and removing any hope of his escape.

It would be a battle to the death. I would avenge our family honor. One of the two of us would die tonight. I recalled the wrestling cage matches I had seen, probably God's provision to prepare me for this moment. I took a deep breath and dove in for the deathblow.

The ogre flew under the door.

He had escaped me.

Not exactly a story to illustrate my courage to my future children.

It's true—I'm not all that adventurous. There aren't Indiana Jones aspirations floating around this mind of mine. So I must have been high on espresso or something when I agreed to hike two cliffs in a single day in Colorado—of all places. This wasn't exactly a day in Disney World. This was a mountain climb, and I should have known we were in trouble from the beginning.

Here's how we almost died.

After a hyperventilating hike, we successfully summited both peaks. It was just as hard as I'd expected. My legs felt as if there were a fire burning from the inside. I was panting so aggressively that it was difficult to take sips of water in between.

A couple of my friends were also nearly a foot taller than me. So I had to walk double-time to keep up. They walked up the mountain, and I jogged to keep up. Not because I wanted to, but because I *had* too.

All of this was like minor-league torture. I was sure al-Qaeda had something to do with it.

The best part of summiting a mountain is knowing that the rest of the hike is downhill. Downhill is good news for a tired, unadventurous, and nonathletic bore.

This was the best part of the day for me. The hike down was the only thing standing between me, flat ground, and a stomachful of hot, fatty, fried food. So, when my friend suggested an alternative, quicker trail down the mountain, I was all ears. If this had been a board meeting, I'd have made the first motion.

They all agreed. They must have wanted food too.

Unfortunately, none of us realized that the "faster" trail, which had long ago been cut into a near-vertical slope on the side of the mountain, had long since been washed down the same mountain by years of snow and rain. The trail started fine. It looked nice and safe, and we started jogging down it. Then, about ten minutes into our trip down, it just vanished. Poof.

So there we were, walking sideways on a vertical slope covered in hundreds of rocks. The rocks and pebbles that blanketed the sandy cliff made it slippery, and if you slipped, you would start sliding down the mountain with nothing to grab on to. You would slide until you died, thousands of feet below.

I figured this danger out just about the moment my friend slipped.

The next few seconds remain imprinted in slow motion on a very sensitive part of my mind. My good friend had *terror* in his eyes as he slowly started to slide down the precipitous cliff. He grasped frantically at the rocks around him. None of them were implanted in the mountain, and each rock he touched went barreling down the slope ahead of him, picking up speed.

We all started screaming.

No doubt with the help of God, we managed to catch our buddy's arm and pull him to safety without losing our own footing.

We sat there in shock, watching the rocks he had dislodged crash, and sometimes explode, at the bottom. Then we looked at the even more hazardous trail ahead of us and decided to backtrack and take the long way down the mountain.

When we reached the spot where our ill-fated trail diverged from the main trail we'd been on, I noticed a wooden sign lying broken on the ground. I picked it up and turned it over. It said, "Warning: This is not a trail. Do not enter."

We later learned that another hiker had recently made the same mistake.

It cost him his life.

BREATHING DIFFERENTLY

We've all had moments when a delicate twist of fate could have caused the tables to turn. We narrowly miss car accidents, we pass by the "wrong place" two minutes before the "wrong time," or we fight for our lives when a common sickness sours into a threat to life.

A few things happen to you after you almost die. The oxygen you're breathing has a certain smell to it. It's almost sweet. You suddenly start to *feel* more deeply. The petty bitterness that you had long harbored in your heart suddenly seems less controlling. The priorities that you believe in so sincerely and that you struggle to adhere to so resiliently suddenly seem easier and simpler to follow. Near-death experiences jar you out of apathy and ingratitude, they realign what you perceive to be most important, and life just—somehow—changes. You learn to actually live that Latin adage: *Seize the day.*

You start to see life through a lens of second chances. The distant, nebulous inevitability of death seems nearer for a little while—sometimes so near you can almost smell its depressing, putrid reality, and each time it's an earthquake to your soul.

This is not a bad feeling. This is a good feeling.

EMBRACING DEATH TO UNDERSTAND LIFE

In traditional cultures, the nearness of death is part of life, according to Dinesh D'Souza, the scholar and author. In modern cultures we tend to embrace an attitude of "full denial" toward death. At all costs, we're committed to keeping death at arm's length. In traditional cultures, "people typically died at home, and a common sight in communities was the funeral procession, a dramatic scene with the body on display and a good deal of conspicuous wailing and shrieking."[1]

This is the way it has been for much of history: people lived acquainted with death. It was a regular part of life, and it influenced how they appreciated the air in their lungs. In modern

America, we not only avoid death at all costs; we don't even speak much of death at our own funerals. We have a closed casket with preachers and friends and family members and sometimes even politicians piling up accolade after accolade about the deceased. They talk nearly exclusively about the life of the person who has died, rather than his death, as a cathartic measure for the mourning masses. Americans spend millions of dollars trying to delay death, and at death we spend thousands more to try to disguise a harsh reality: all that is good about life and this world is running inevitably toward a cold, barren, and often unexpected end.

D'Souza, referencing the work of another author, puts it this way:

> The West has developed an elaborate procedure for "hushing up" death. In America and Europe, people no longer die at home, in full view of the family; they die in hospitals, cut off from the world around them. Even family members just visit; they don't experience death up close. In the final scene of this arid drama, the doctor comes in and solemnly informs you, "He's passed away," or "He's gone." Euphemisms abound; they don't even have the courage to say, "He is dead." . . .
>
> People in the West go to funerals out of a sense of obligation, but no one wants to go. It is discomforting to see a dead body in a casket. We don't like to be put through this, and we can't wait to get out of there and back to our normal life. . . . In the West, people don't die; they just disappear.[2]

I've noticed these divergent perspectives on death a number of times on my journeys with college students around the world.

In the impoverished places of our globe, where death is always close, I've seen students near panic after their sheltered views of life and death have been shattered by the sight in passing of a dying beggar on the side of the road or a poor child whose lack of access to medical care has caused an easily curable tumor to grow to a size larger than its host.

A raw run-in with death is a traumatizing experience for Westerners because we so rarely encounter it—and when we do encounter it, we find it in its most domesticated form.

Death is to us a tame lion. As a result, we have lost the ability to really value and appreciate *life*.

This, perhaps, is why we're so little affected by the revolutionary words of Jesus: "Whoever hears my word and believes him who sent me has eternal life and will not be judged but has crossed over from *death to life*."[3]

Or as the humanist and essayist William Hazlitt has written, oddly enough: "Death cancels everything but truth."[4]

JESUS HAS RESCUED US

Christianity grew up in a traditional culture very well acquainted with death, and this is why the doctrine of resurrection was such a potent salve to the early Christians during their suffering. Aside from living in a world with a life expectancy of thirty years or less, those who lived in that society faced all kinds of natural maladies, like diseases with no cures and the constant threat of wars. The Christians also struggled to stay alive in a perilous time for enemies, perceived or otherwise, of the Roman Empire. Christians valued the doctrine of resurrection because it provided them with hope and grace and love and peace even in the midst of turbulence and anxiety and threats of all kinds on every side.

The doctrine of resurrection was the IV that fed the faith of those early Christians when they didn't have the strength to feed themselves. Because of this belief they were "hard pressed on every side, but not crushed; perplexed, but not in despair; persecuted, but not abandoned; struck down, but not destroyed."[5] They simply knew that "the one who raised the Lord Jesus from the dead will also raise us with Jesus."[6]

This was a startlingly countercultural belief for the Romans.

The Romans had adopted the philosophy of the Greeks into their religious system, meaning that almost no one seriously believed in an afterlife. But to the Christians, a belief in the afterlife influenced the here and now. They believed that Jesus had rescued them from the inevitability of death. They viewed their faith as a life preserver in the turbulence of this world. They lived in the shadow of death, but they knew that Jesus, because of his grace, had rescued them from it. He had given them the greatest gift in the world. They understood the power of this gift, and they lived in the knowledge and light of that power.

They viewed what we refer to as *salvation* as so much more than a tamed religious vocabulary word. Jesus had literally *rescued* them by bringing them from death to life. *He reached down and pulled them up just as they were sliding down their own cliff toward death.*

They thought of Jesus the way we think of a fireman rescuing a child from a house crackling and exploding in flames. They thought of Jesus the way we think of a lifeguard pulling a drowning man from the tumbling ocean. Salvation was to them like a Green Beret rescuing a captured soldier from a bloodthirsty mob. It was a powerful, meaningful, rescuing experience.

But the work of Jesus didn't end there. God rescued them— then he also restored, renewed, and reconciled their relationship with God. Jesus pulled them from the flames and the waves, and he reunited them with their estranged heavenly Father.

Grace is the great rescuing of God's people, by God, from *death* to *life*.

HAVING GOTTEN GRACE, WE SHOULD GIVE GRACE

Yet, from the very beginning, Jesus' expectation was that grace was not something to be hoarded, but something to be shared. It was good news worth telling, and it is our responsibility, and our privilege, to tell the world about the kindness of God, the forgiveness of our sins, and the opportunity to become members of his kingdom. This was so important to Jesus that he shouted it down to them as he ascended to heaven after his resurrection. He told them to go tell the world the good news that God has made a way for man to know God again. And in his telling, he gave them very specific instructions. He told them to start where they were in Jerusalem and then go to Judea and then to the entire world.

The resurrected one was granting his followers the opportunity to bring resurrection to others. It was our joy to tell them the good news, to help them find what they've been looking for, maybe for their entire lives.

Grace isn't just to be received. It's also meant to be given.

It's like that particular Christmas when my parents gave me the gift I never expected to receive. I wanted it so badly—I dreamed about it, begged for it, but I never imagined I would actually get it.

When I stumbled out early that Christmas Day to discover that they had left it right there for me with a big red bow on it, I just stared at it in disbelief for a little while. I thought I was still dreaming, or I had burrowed into my imagination again.

But it was real.

It was there, staring at me in living color.

My next reaction was a little less dignified.

I totally freaked out. I started screaming and running around the room in a frenzy of joy. I jumped on the couch and clapped my hands and started to go absolutely crazy in view of my whole family. Surely, the entire neighborhood heard the racket as I went absolutely insane with my gratitude. I wanted the whole planet to know that I had received the greatest gift in the world.

I imagine my parents started to wonder if their Christmas present had finally pushed me over the edge. It was time to go to the child psychologist again.

There's a YouTube video that my friends and I have watched over and over of a kid receiving, like me, the Christmas present he'd always wanted. That kid's response put even my childhood reaction to shame. I thought the poor kid was going to have a heart attack. I almost had a secondhand heart attack watching him.

Have you ever seen someone totally lose his mind in celebration?

That is the appropriate reaction when Jesus' grace comes alive in your heart—when it hits you that he has brought you from *death to life*. It's a kind of joy and celebration that cannot be contained.

It's like swallowing an atomic bomb.

The natural reaction is a frenzy of gratitude. The second natural reaction is to start telling people about it, and the next is to start modeling grace in your own life.

Just think about it for a minute.

There you were, like my friend, sliding down the mountain toward an inevitable, sudden abyss when Jesus reached down and rescued you, bringing you from *death to life*. He came at the right moment, perhaps even at the last second, and he left you not only with air in your lungs, but with a new kind of life—a life where nearness to God is as common as breathing and eating. A life lived with God in perpetual joy.

At this very moment, as I type these words in a little café downtown in my tiny little town, I can see again my friends and me standing at the head of that trail in Colorado. I can feel again the mixed feelings of regret as we stared at the fallen sign we'd missed, for being so stupid, but also an overwhelming gratitude for the feeling of *new life* that washed over me as I stood there, having been brought from death to life.

We were, at that moment, in the first act of our second chance.

In some sense, we all stand in the same place as recipients of a grace we did not deserve. And yet often, tragically, rather than being overwhelmed with gratitude, we've forgotten how close we came to death.

Somehow, it's this reality that compels us to move from being recipients of grace to distributors of it. We can't keep it to ourselves. We feel a privilege and a responsibility to climb to the tower in the center of town and scream at the top of our lungs into the distant mountains:

"I have good news! God cares for you!"

In return, God echoes, "The good news of grace is yours, and it's yours to give."

It's our responsibility to be to others what Jesus has been to us.

We get the chance to tell people who feel dead that Jesus still moves tombstones.

ELEVEN

WHAT TO DO WHEN TERRORISTS KILL YOUR SPOUSE

GRACE ISN'T FLASHY.

It's not accompanied by fanfare and fireworks.

It's not sexy or flamboyant.

It rarely draws much attention, and it's not usually celebrated, even though it deserves to be. Grace is seen in less conspicuous ways: in the kindness of a good boss or the quiet generosity of a secret gift. It's evident in a gentle response delivered to an angry driver, or in the person who simply chooses to overlook the fault of someone who really deserves a piece of your mind. It's found in sacrificing the little you have for the good of others, and by treating people not as they deserve but as God has treated you.

The premise of this book is that God's relationship with people is primarily defined as a relationship of grace, and grace should make us better people and make the world a better place. It's our responsibility as God's children to live as people of grace in a world that desperately needs what it doesn't always accept.

Why is grace not always accepted? Because it comes from a value system different from the one governing this world. It's the antithesis of the thirst for power that compels so many people to work so hard and to climb to the top by stepping on those they pass on the way. Grace is the enemy of *looking out for number one* and *survival of the fittest.*

Grace treats people precisely *not* as they deserve. We might be willing to give second chances, but grace gives seventh chances. Grace is an ethic from heaven that governs the lives of people who love Jesus.

The most powerful example of grace I've heard was the story of a little German widow whose husband was among the two Turkish pastors and a German missionary tortured to death by radical Muslims in April 2007.

The Muslims had feigned interest in Christianity after attending an Easter service and had scheduled an appointment for more information with the pastors. Each of the radical Muslims arrived at the appointment with a bag of makeshift torture devices under his arm.

When they arrived at the small room for their meeting with the Christians, they locked the door, then took their time taking apart the "infidels" for their heresy, piece by piece.

The widow of the German missionary was left with three beautiful, blue-eyed children. Her husband was slaughtered by the very people they had come to serve, and she was faced now with hard decisions about her future.

People from around the world, including many of her compatriots in Turkey, put enormous pressure on her to leave the mission field and return to a safer place to raise her children alone. They compelled her to leave the dangerous work that she and her husband had committed their lives to, and to come to a safer place.

Instead, this widow told a national Turkish paper:

We have been in Malatya for over ten years now, everyone respected and cared for us. I want to forgive my husband's assassins because I believe they don't know what they have done. My husband was killed in the name of Jesus Christ, and because of his love of Him. We want to go on living here, my children go to school here and I want my husband to be buried here in the city cemetery, so my son can go and place flowers on his grave and in doing so draw strength to go on hoping and believing.[1]

In those sincere and courageous words we see the power of grace. Grace that sees past logic, grace that embraces a near-supernatural forgiveness, and grace that believes that God still can take terrorists like Saul and make them Paul.

Some people might think this dear widow is insane for staying in the city where her husband was brutally murdered. They would say that she should hate these men who made her a widow and took her children's father. They might call her insane—but no one would call her weak. Only a powerful person can let grace triumph over hate and still believe when life seems beyond belief.

That's the power of grace, and that's real power.

WHICH POWER WILL YOU CHOOSE?

The power of grace and the power of this world are at odds with one another. One sees power in self-preservation at all costs, and the other sees power in self-sacrifice, but each of these divergent systems of belief draws upon a god for their strength.

Grace, as you must know by now, comes from Jesus, its author.

The power of grace, the ability to live as a person of grace, comes from him. When you've submitted to Jesus as your guide in life, and when you're plugged into him as your source, when his teachings are your guide, and he is the God that you worship, you'll find yourself naturally inclined to live a life of grace. You'll have the *power* to live the way he would live if he were in your shoes. You'll have a sense of the way he would make your decisions and how he would react in your life's situations.

You'll eventually become a person who naturally exudes grace.

If your life is lived in worship of a different god, which Christians refer to as idolatry, then you'll find yourself naturally inclined to live a life governed by the god you worship. Grace cannot coexist with idolatry because the ability to live a life of grace, to react in our lives the way that dear German widow reacted in Turkey, is a supernatural gift granted to us by God. We *have* to be plugged into our relationship with him in order to have the power to live as he's designed us to live.

A person is like this laptop I'm typing on. It has a battery with a limited life span. So do we. After a little while, if I don't get it plugged into the source of its power, it'll trickle into nothing. So do we. The battery will be drained. It will have no more power to give. If I never connect it to the source again, it will die.

Guess what? So will we. Our ability to live life well is contingent upon being plugged into our source—and that source is a growing relationship with the living God, through Jesus Christ.

C. S. Lewis said it this way:

> What Satan put into the heads of our remote ancestors was the idea that they could "be like gods"—could set up on their own as if they had created themselves—be their own masters—invent

some sort of happiness for themselves outside God, apart from God. And out of that hopeless attempt has come nearly all that we call human history—money, poverty, ambition, war, prostitution, classes, empires, slavery—the long terrible story of man trying to find something other than God which will make him happy.

The reason why it can never succeed is this. God made us: invented us as a man invents an engine. A car is made to run on petrol, and it would not run properly on anything else. Now God designed the human machine to run on Himself. He Himself is the fuel our spirits were designed to burn, or the food our spirits were designed to feed on. There is no other. That is why it is just no good asking God to make us happy in our own way without bothering about religion. God cannot give us a happiness and peace apart from Himself, because it is not there. There is no such thing.[2]

We weren't meant to live independent of our source of life. We were meant to live tethered to our source of life. He created us with an internal image of him that is accurate enough that it enables us to learn to mimic him. That's how we become people who live lives of grace.

Since the moment Adam and Eve attempted to subvert the authority of God, the human race has had the power cord yanked out of the socket, and we're working against the clock. The battery is draining, the clock is ticking, and we're trying to hydrate our souls with castor oil. We keep plugging ourselves into dead sockets, and we somehow run in every direction but the right one. Meanwhile, God is accessible and grace is free. We're like thirsty people living next to a waterfall of pure, crystal clear, healthy water, but for some reason every time we're thirsty, we run off to the nearest bar and drink poison.

The first step to living a life empowered by grace is ensuring that we remain plugged into the source, that we've eradicated the idols from our lives that war for our affection. We have to stop trying to find every way in the world to preserve our independence from God. We have to stop trying to straddle the fence between the God of grace and the gods of this world.

Tim Keller has described the kinds of "counterfeit gods" that rob us of the opportunity to live a life of grace:

> It can be family and children, or career and making money, or achievement and critical acclaim, or saving "face" and social standing. It can be a romantic relationship, peer approval, competence and skill, secure and comfortable circumstances, your beauty or your brains, a great political or social cause, your morality and virtue, or even success in Christian ministry. When your meaning in life is to fix someone else's life, we may call it "co-dependency" but it is really idolatry. An idol is whatever you look at and say, in your heart of hearts, "If I have that, then I'll feel my life has meaning, then I'll know I have value, then I'll be significant and secure."[3]

THE SERIOUSNESS OF THIS THREAT

What's most unfortunate is that most of the time, down deep inside, we actually don't believe this is a very big deal. We think of idolatry in the same way we think of telling little white lies. It's like stealing a pen from the office or participating in a little bit of gossip. It's wrong—but not *very* wrong. Not enough to worry about. It's a sin we tolerate so that we're not tempted to try other, more egregious sins.

Actually, this vice, above all others, has grieved God the most through the centuries. It has cost the people of God more than any other sin, and it has robbed the world of all kinds of goodness that should have resulted from the lives of those plugged into a relationship with the author of grace.

Scripture reserves the most vivid words ever spoken by God to his people to address idolatry, and idolatry is the sin most often repeated in the biblical story.

Hosea, for instance, wrote,

> When Israel was a child, I loved him, and out of Egypt I called my son. But the more I called Israel, the further they went from me. They sacrificed to the Baals and they burned incense to images. It was I who taught Ephraim to walk, taking them by the arms; but they did not realize it was I who healed them.[4]

Notice the passionate, frank language God used to confront his people in Ezekiel 16 for their idolatry:

> On the day you were born your umbilical cord was not cut, you weren't bathed and cleaned up, you weren't rubbed with salt, you weren't wrapped in a baby blanket. No one cared a fig for you. No one did one thing to care for you tenderly in these ways. You were thrown out into a vacant lot and left there, dirty and unwashed—a newborn nobody wanted.
>
> And then I came by. I saw you all miserable and bloody. Yes, I said to you, lying there helpless and filthy, "Live! Grow

up like a plant in the field!" And you did. You grew up. You grew tall and matured as a woman, full-breasted, with flowing hair. But you were naked and vulnerable, fragile and exposed.

I came by again and saw you, saw that you were ready for love and a lover. I took care of you, dressed you and protected you. I promised you my love and entered the covenant of marriage with you. I, GOD, the Master, gave my word. You became mine. I gave you a good bath, washing off all that old blood, and anointed you with aromatic oils. I dressed you in a colorful gown and put leather sandals on your feet. I gave you linen blouses and a fashionable wardrobe of expensive clothing. I adorned you with jewelry: I placed bracelets on your wrists, fitted you out with a necklace, emerald rings, sapphire earrings, and a diamond tiara. You were provided with everything precious and beautiful: with exquisite clothes and elegant food, garnished with honey and oil. You were absolutely stunning. You were a queen! You became world-famous, a legendary beauty brought to perfection by my adornments. . . .

But your beauty went to your head and you became a common whore, grabbing anyone coming down the street and taking him into your bed. You took your fine dresses and made "tents" of them, using them as brothels in which you practiced your trade. This kind of thing should never happen, never.

And then you took all that fine jewelry I gave you, my gold and my silver, and made pornographic images of them for your brothels. You decorated your beds with fashionable silks and cottons, and perfumed them with my aromatic oils and incense. And then you set out the wonderful foods

I provided—the fresh breads and fruits, with fine herbs and spices, which were my gifts to you—and you served them as delicacies in your whorehouses. That's what happened, says GOD, the Master.

And then you took your sons and your daughters, whom you had given birth to as my children, and you killed them, sacrificing them to idols. Wasn't it bad enough that you had become a whore? And now you're a murderer, killing my children and sacrificing them to idols.

Not once during these years of outrageous obscenities and whorings did you remember your infancy, when you were naked and exposed, a blood-smeared newborn. (vv. 4–22 MSG)

And this is just the beginning. There are dozens of verses citing God's frustration and brokenheartedness over his people's idolatry and their ingratitude for his grace.

———

The first step to a lifestyle of grace is identifying the specific gods who represent the greatest threat to living that life of grace. Otherwise, you'll find, as the prophet Jonah has written, that "those who cling to worthless idols forfeit the grace that could be theirs."[5]

Identifying your idol of choice is not very difficult. Just look into your daydreams and observe your daily life, and ask yourself these questions:

1. What brings me the most satisfaction and security in life?
2. What is it that, if I had it, would solve all my problems?

3. If I could snap my fingers and make anything reality,
   what would it be?
4. What do I think I can't live without?

The answers to these questions will reveal the idol that threatens you.

Then you must, with all your might and with the help of God, put that in its proper place: second to Jesus.

TWELVE

GLADLY STRANGE

Grace is mainly lived out in little ways. In the daily decisions we make, in the values we profess, in what we fight for and what we concede, and in how we treat our friends—and our enemies.

Occasionally, grace is tested in more overt ways, when everything in us makes us want to follow a different path. In those situations, eventually, hopefully, grace proves itself more powerful than our desire for wrath or revenge or looking out for number one or preserving our image at all costs.

In both the minute and the grandiose, grace has always treated people better than they deserve, and it has always been what sets followers of Jesus Christ apart.

Grace is radical, and it's meant to be lived in radical ways.

Grace is unorthodox. When it is a part of someone's life, it should cause others to wonder why this person is behaving this way. Someone who lives a lifestyle of grace should seem to live out a different ethic.

The early Christian leaders and apostles taught us that Christians should be "in the world but not of it." We should consider ourselves sojourners, journeying through life on earth to our real home in heaven. We are pilgrims, aliens, and residents of another place. All of these concepts suggest that this isn't our home, and people should look at us as a "peculiar" people, the "children of God" traveling through planet Earth.

Christians should never blend in. Our lives themselves should preach our loudest sermon.

These days Christians probably don't blend in, but it's not the same kind of peculiarity that Jesus had in mind. We shouldn't be different because of our idiosyncrasies, our famous leaders, our political opinions, or our worship styles. We should seem different in a more nuanced sense: we should seem different because we are living out what we believe in a way that causes others to wonder what curious belief undergirds our lifestyle. We should look out for those in need, we should forsake the dog-eat-dog mentality of modern society in exchange for servant leadership, and we should care about people the way Jesus cared about us.

Instead, many of those around us think we're different because of the "product" we peddle or the policies we preach.

These things certainly have their appropriate place in our Christian identity, but Jesus had a much more clandestine, supernatural form of "distinctiveness" in mind. He didn't want his followers to stand out as walking billboards, their T-shirts painted with clichés and Bible verses. He didn't envision us building the largest buildings in small towns and marching on Capitol Hill. Jesus expected us to be different, but not in the sense of an ugly duckling, or a bright orange house in a row of white ones. He imagined our difference as having more substance, a more subversive quality, and greater effectiveness.

For instance, imagine two identical cars. Both are black with sleek body styles. They are freshly painted with racing stripes running down their sides, the same tires and rims, the same shape, size, and design. But there is one distinct difference—the engine. One car has a refurbished engine that a mechanic pried out of a dying Ford Pinto in a salvage shop. The other has a newly minted Porsche engine.

Within ten seconds of riding in either of these vehicles, you would discover that something was drastically different between the two. The car with the Porsche engine would accelerate more smoothly and more quickly. The difference might not be noticeable from the outside, but one test drive would make it abundantly clear that these two cars were different.

This is how Christians should be different.

We dress the same way and live in the same culture, but there's just something radically different—or at least there should be—about how we operate on the road of life. We have values and beliefs, a philosophy of life, and a motivation for doing good that are distinctly different from the world around us.

We are in the world, but not of it.

I love how Gerald Sittser, the theologian and historian, described how this sense of living differently *within* culture fueled Christianity's early explosion from an embryonic Jewish sect to a faith known across the Roman Empire, within a single generation:

> How did the Christian movement create a sense of belonging that made people feel included, loved and cared for? First, the Christian community welcomed outsiders, regardless of their background, and thus overcame the obvious divisions of gender, ethnicity and class that characterized the Roman world. As the apologist Tatian noted, the church seemed to include everyone, making no "distinctions in rank and outward appearance, or

wealth and education, or age and sex." Christians maintained close contact with family, friends, neighbors and coworkers, which provided a large pool of potential converts who found the small but vital movement attractive. Living mostly in cities, Christians bartered in the same markets, drew water from the same wells, worked in the same shops and lived in the same kinds of apartments as everyone else. They did not use organized rallies, high-profile evangelists and big-budget programs to win recruits. If anything, Christians maintained a low profile to avoid public notice. The church thus attracted outsiders through natural networks of relationships. . . . [The philosopher Celsus] noted that Christians won converts not through public debate among elites but through quiet witness in their homes and places of work.[1]

Christians taught their theology and introduced people to their unique path to God by demonstrating how their faith affected their lives *within* culture. They were people who had received grace, and they lived under the conviction that they should live as people of grace *within* culture and not *outside* of it.

This is what Jesus had in mind when he prayed to his Father in John 17, "Father, I'm not asking that you take them out of the world, but you leave them in the world and be with them in the world."

GRACE AND LOVE MAKE YOU LOSE YOUR MIND

Christians are a peculiar people precisely because they are recipients of the grace of God, and they are in turn emissaries of that grace to their communities and their families, to their employers and employees, to their friends and to the fatherless, the widowed, and the orphaned. They are the trumpeters of a new reality where God and man can coexist in harmony with one another again, and where love is demonstrated in a way so countercultural that many people do not understand what they are seeing.

Grace is inherently radical because grace chooses to ignore what might be deserved and to dole out mercy instead.

Most of the time, grace is most evident in the small things and in everyday moments. It's evident in how we respond in the office when someone treats us unjustly. It's visible in the little decisions we make when faced with an opportunity to serve ourselves or someone else. It's evident in the practice of virtues like hospitality, patience, kindness, goodness, and self-control. It's visible when we run upon someone in need at the most inopportune moment, or at times when we have every reason in the world to retaliate and, instead, we turn the other cheek.

But on occasion, in a rare and probably difficult moment, grace must rise to a higher place. It must exhibit itself in a more extravagant form, a form more akin to the way in which grace waged war against sin on the cross.

It's in these moments that the world around us sees more clearly that our values are from another place where the rules are different, and where selflessness seems to actually hold sway over self-interest.

These are the moments when men and women see the gospel in living color through our lives, and where we discover for ourselves how much of Jesus is *really* inside of us.

Recently, I read a story that clearly demonstrates this otherworldly kind of grace. It's not easy for me to even write about it, because it runs so starkly against everything in my human nature. Even so—or maybe precisely because of that—it illustrates the power of a profound belief in the grace of God and of how that belief can run so deeply in the human heart that it is, in itself, a miracle.

GRACE IN NICKEL MINES

On the morning of October 5, 2006, twenty-five children were studying in the local one-room schoolhouse, a barnlike structure with a simple bell tower and a front porch supported by steel rods. The building, as plain as notebook paper, reflected the values of the Amish community that educated its children there. The Amish trace their lineage back to pacifist Swiss Christian communities, who, during the sixteenth and seventeenth centuries, renounced the trappings of worldliness.

On that morning, in the midst of the Amish, the worst of the world's madness appeared. At 9:51 a.m., Charles Carl Roberts IV, a thirty-two-year-old milkman, burst into the West Nickel Mines Amish schoolhouse and shattered the community's serenity. He had thought about the violence he was about to perpetrate long in advance, and he came prepared. He carried a 12-gauge shotgun, a 9 mm handgun, a .30-06 bolt-action rifle, about six hundred rounds of ammunition, a stun gun, and two knives. He also had tools and building supplies with him.

He ordered the young girls to line up quickly in front of the chalkboard. Then he demanded that the teacher, Emma Mae Zook, take her fifteen male students, a pregnant woman, and three mothers with infants outside. Once they were gone, Charles Roberts used the tools and the 2 x 6 and 2 x 4 foot boards he was carrying to barricade himself inside. Next, he used flex ties to bind the hands and legs of the young girls, who ranged in age from six to thirteen.

Evidently he meant to take his time. He called his wife on a cell phone to confess, in partial explanation of the suicide notes he had left at home, that he had molested two young relatives twenty years before. This tale seems to have been a delusion. He also spoke of his grief at the death of an infant daughter. When the Amish girls asked Roberts why he meant to hurt them, he said he was angry at God.

The community responded more quickly than Roberts may have anticipated, and the schoolgirls themselves would alter his plans. Roberts's plan to molest the girls seems apparent from the lubricant he was carrying, but their teacher, Emma Mae Zook, ran to a neighboring farmhouse and called the police at 10:36 a.m. The police arrived in force nine minutes later. From the loudspeakers on their cruisers they spoke to Roberts. He responded that if the grounds weren't cleared in two seconds he'd kill everyone.

The oldest of the girls, Marian Fisher, spoke up. The Amish speak Swiss German as their mother tongue, but she used the best English she could muster. She pleaded, "Shoot me and leave the others one's [sic] loose." Marian's eleven-year-old sister, Barbie, asked to be next. They demonstrated the greatest love a human possibly could.

Unnerved by the girls' courage and the police, Roberts tried to execute all ten girls, pouring bullets into them as fast as he could.

At the sound of the gunfire the police rushed the building. With one final blast, Roberts committed suicide before they could reach him.

Although Roberts shot all ten children at point blank range, and several of them repeatedly, he did not fully exact the revenge against God he had planned. Five children survived. Marian's sister, Barbie, was one of them, which is why we know some of the details of what happened inside the schoolhouse that horrible day.

Charles Roberts's death seemed sad only in that he was no longer available to prosecute.

But that's where this story turns in an unexpected direction. The entire Amish community followed young Marian Fisher's lead of sacrifice and love of one's neighbor. While Charles Roberts chose to unleash his anger on the innocent, the Amish chose to bestow forgiveness on the guilty. Newsreel footage showed the Amish horse-and-buggy cortege rolling along the main road in Nickel Mines on their way to the funerals of slain children. It was a poignant and picturesque scene. But the images that stayed in the imagination were of the Amish men and women attending Charles Roberts's funeral in the graveyard of his wife's Methodist church. They insisted it was not their place to judge him. Amish leaders even asked their community to refrain from thinking of Roberts as evil.

The Amish also reached out to Marie Roberts and her children. They invited the family to attend the girls' funerals—for the Bible says to mourn with those who mourn, and the Roberts family was mourning their own loss. As money poured in to address the medical bills of the wounded girls,

Amish community leaders stipulated that a fund be set up from these resources to take care of the killer's widow and three children.[2]

The Nickel Mines community responded with true grace—totally undeserved, unmerited, and crosslike grace.

For most of us, this is just *too* free, *too* forgiving, and *too* unmerited. We struggle with the *people-should-get-what-they-deserve* mentality that is not necessarily sinful, but can, nevertheless, rob us of the opportunity to truly experience what Jesus experienced for us on the cross.

This world doesn't operate on the principle of grace, and that's partly what makes Jesus' gift to us so absurd. It's why nearly everyone looks upon the story of the Nickel Mines as possessing a kind of peculiarity first seen in Jesus' own death upon the cross.

It's also what makes the kingdom of God so drastically different from a world that operates on the law of retribution and that demands reciprocal justice, eye for an eye and tooth for a tooth.

It's my struggle, just as it's your struggle. But *should* it be a struggle for those of us who have been freed and forgiven by the undeserving death of Jesus upon a cross for our sins?

I wouldn't insist that the reaction of the Amish at Nickel Mines should be normative. I would have almost certainly responded differently, but as I read the story of their reaction, I couldn't help but experience a crisis of faith. Because, in some sense, the tragic, horrifying, and disgusting story of Roberts and the strange, almost alien reaction of the Amish community are together a very clear depiction of the emotions and ridiculousness of the gospel. We are Roberts—and yet God has given us a kind of mercy we never deserved. While I'm not a pacifist, I can't help but admire the total, literal application of the doctrine of grace applied by these dear, hurting people.

When I read this story, my sense was that these people had a kind of value system that isn't from this planet. They are radicals—because they actually live what they believe.

But, maybe, responses such as that should be more normative than most of us are willing to admit. True grace is so radical that it causes an earthquake to our sense of the normal—to what is meant by *common sense*. Common sense wouldn't have changed the world through the death of the Son of God on a Roman cross.

BREAKING THE ADDICTION TO LOOKING GOOD

Most of us will never experience such a radical test of our faith. Yet this harrowing story of totally committed faith ought to convict us to live lives of grace in the far lesser challenges that we face day to day. If these men and woman could exhibit such inextinguishable love in such a tragic moment, then surely we can stand in the gap for those in our world and around the world who need grace, whether that grace is deserved or not.

The world should somehow be a better place because it's filled with people who love Jesus and who want to follow in his example.

THIRTEEN

——

GOD MIGHT WANT YOU TO FAIL YOUR TEST

SOMETIMES OUR IDEA OF GRACE WRONGLY reduces our view of God. We relegate him to the place of a passive-aggressive, effeminate grandmother who can't help but give her little grandbabies what they want when they want it whether or not they deserve it. God suddenly seems easily taken advantage of. We can manipulate him to give us what we want over what we deserve.

This is not only a heretical view of God and of grace, but it oversimplifies grace and is personally damaging to our relationships with God and others. Grace is free, but it's not always easy. Sometimes, the most gracious thing God can do for us, or we can do for others, stings a little in the end.

If I'm going to write an honest book on grace, then I have to tell you that God sometimes practices "tough grace" that, while it might give us what we *need* over what we *deserve*, is painful too. Grace is not weak—it's meek. And the most needed kind of grace is sometimes the *most difficult* to bear.

It's like the doctor who chooses to break your bone again in order to set it properly so that it grows back as it's supposed to, as opposed to the doctor who doesn't want to cause you any more pain and therefore chooses to knowingly let that broken bone of yours heal in an imperfect way.

God is more than willing to cause you pain now in order to bring you peace . . . later.

OUR ENTITLEMENT ATTITUDE TOWARD GOD

You can always tell if you believe, down deep inside, that God should always make your life easy and lavish loads of soft grace on you. You'll know it when you catch yourself saying these five words: "God, this just isn't fair!"

When God gives us tough grace (by *not* stepping in and helping us or by helping us in a way we don't expect), we appeal to some cosmic sense of fairness, failing to realize that the absolute last thing we want from God is for him to treat us fairly. Treating us fairly—meaning treating us as we deserve—wouldn't have given us any grace at all. Fairness would have forbidden our redemption.

God is always kind to us, but sometimes his kindness comes in the form of a kick in the pants—and when it does, we sometimes feel as if he's treating us unfairly because we feel *entitled to our rights.*

Listen, I'm an expert at this.

I work with college students (at Liberty University—the world's largest Christian university), and I'm in the unusual place of also being within the same generation, or social demographic, as those I teach. At least, for now, we're all millennials (along with eighty million other Americans born after 1980), and I can testify (and so do the stats) that we are among the most entitled generations in history. Our culture and our families and even our churches have taught us that we deserve to be treated in a certain way. We feel entitled to success and money and opportunity and *grace*, and we drag this sense of entitlement into every stage of our life from college to children (we're not old enough yet to be grandparents!). We expect to be, and we believe we deserve to be, treated a certain way, and we think we deserve chance after chance after chance even if we don't intend on changing anything.

This is glaringly apparent in my work with students.

Every year about midsemester, I notice a sharp spike in the student body's prayer life. Suspiciously, about the time midterms are coming due, students start praying more intently and showing up in church more frequently, and the God-talk on campus goes up a notch or two. It doesn't matter that they've habitually skipped class all semester, or that they've so frequently fallen asleep in class that they've begun to bring rags in their book bags to wipe the drool off their desks. They're not even sure they know the name of the professor anymore—and then, suddenly, they have an epiphany: "Wow, college is expensive, and I'm not here to play video games and intramural sports and date every night of the week. I'm here to get an education."

Then they try to straighten up. They decide to get serious—two months too late.

They ask the professors for a little extra help; they befriend a geek in class who can help them sharpen their math or history or science skills. They maneuver to get into a group project with the smartest kids in class, and they even go ahead and purchase their textbooks from the bookstore.

They get so serious that they no longer return to their dorm rooms for their sacred five-hour afternoon naps. Instead, they go to the library with a pile of books about the history of the world and microbiology, and they determine to sharpen their minds during naptime instead of just letting them atrophy. In fact, they even schedule their appointments with their math tutors for after their study time in the library so it looks to the tutors as though they are actually studious.

Then the tutor shows up for the appointment and *hears* his budding scholar even before he sees him. That's because he's snoring, and it's one of those train-whistle kinds of snores, in the sacred university library, of all places. Suddenly, the kid wakes up, glances mortified at his tutor, rustles his stuff together, and says something crazy about having to get close to the page because he can't see the page from far away. The only problem is that he's been lying on the book for so long that it has formed indentations in his forehead. Fail.

When it becomes clear that this flurry of last-minute effort isn't going to do the trick, what's left for the desperate scholar to use to pull the semester out of the fire?

Jesus!

Jesus, of course! He can do anything, right?

Jesus is a God of grace, right? And, boy, do I need some grace! I'm entitled to grace. Besides, he's a nice guy.

Suddenly, the most spiritually apathetic kid in the school decides he's going to fast for the first time in his life. For the next twenty-four hours, there will be no McDonald's, no cafeteria buffets, and, God forbid, no ramen noodles (unless, of course, he just drinks the flavored water).

He's going to *truly beg* God for grace, and God's going to give it to him because that's how God is. *He's a nice guy and he loves the whole world (including losers), and that means he'll help me.*

So, our student prays and prays and prays.

And fails his test . . .

. . . because God isn't his grandma.

REAL GRACE IS NOT CHEAP GRACE

We all have a tendency to ignore what we know we *must* do, choosing instead what we *want* to do, and then expect God to somehow deposit in our minds the information we didn't study, or deposit in our bank accounts the money we have already spent, or reinstate the love we've already lost. We beg God for grace, and, down deep inside, we really expect him to give us grace every time—because, after all, our God is a God of grace, right?

Unfortunately, this perception of grace, sometimes prevalent in the church, fuels the primary misperceptions our culture has of God.

Plenty of people these days view God as a benevolent grandpa, always ready and waiting to bail his grandkids out if they get into trouble. Others view God as a divine vending machine whose primary purpose is to dole out the blessings we want and need in response to the currency of good deeds that we deposit. Some people think of God as a spare tire, always sitting there patiently in the wings of life, just waiting hopefully, ready for someone to need him.

It's our cheapening of grace that has caused these cultural ideas of God to not only grow at an astounding rate, but to even infiltrate our churches and our pastors' views of, and teachings about, God. This heresy of cheap, meaningless grace is one of the most dangerous illnesses within the body of Christ today.

It causes us to forget that grace always costs something, and that grace is a means to an end, but it's not the end in and of itself. Grace is always given with the hope that it will *bring* something, like restoration or redemption, or that it will catalyze some kind of change in the life of the recipient.

Grace is a down payment on future transformation.

Even the judge who extends grace to someone convicted by the court is doing so not to diminish the importance of the law, but in the hope that his generosity will persuade the guilty one to embrace what's right over what's wrong *next time*. God gives us grace in the hope that his kindness will draw us to repentance, and a boss gives an employee grace in the hope that he'll change if given a second chance. "I think he's learned his lesson," that boss might say.

I suspect that the Christian leader and author who wrote most profoundly about the tragic abuse of grace, which he called "cheap grace," was the German pastor Dietrich Bonhoeffer. Here's what he said:

Cheap grace is the deadly enemy of our Church. We are fighting to-day for costly grace.

Cheap grace means grace sold on the market like cheapjacks' wares. The sacraments, the forgiveness of sin, and the consolations of religion are thrown away at cut prices. Grace is represented as the Church's inexhaustible treasury, from which she showers blessings with generous hands, without asking questions or fixing limits. Grace without price; grace without cost! The essence of grace, we suppose, is that the account has

136

been paid in advance; and, because it has been paid, everything can be had for nothing. Since the cost was infinite, the possibilities of using and spending it are infinite. What would grace be if it were not cheap? . . . Cheap grace is the preaching of forgiveness without requiring repentance, baptism without church discipline, Communion without confession, absolution without personal confession. Cheap grace is grace without discipleship, grace without the cross, grace without Jesus Christ, living and incarnate.[1]

Sound familiar?

Of course, no Christian in his right mind would *say* that this is the right way of handling grace, but in practice, I think plenty of us are guilty of *living* this way. It becomes an attitude we nurse toward God, or the way we live out our interactions with him. While God has welcomed us into his family, shown us extravagant love, and given us bottomless grace, he is also still God. He can still pulverize the planet with the blink of an eye. Just because he's welcomed us *to boldly come into the throne of grace in our time of need*, it doesn't mean that we should barge in like we own the place.

We should respect and fear him.

Instead, we sometimes take our grace and we run. We abuse grace knowing that God will forgive us again. We choose to live in a way that takes advantage of the kindness of God. That attacks the very core of our relationship with God by diminishing in our lives God's nature and his character. We begin to think of him weakly, and we start to live as if he doesn't matter.

The seriousness of this is most evident when you consider the historical context within which Bonhoeffer's concern about cheap grace was conceived.

Bonhoeffer was a pastor in Germany during the era when Hitler took over the nation and led it into war with the entire world. Hitler's Nazi regime sought out the eradication of all Jews from the planet. Millions were murdered during the Holocaust, and today Hitler's name remains among the most infamous in world history. He is universally believed to be an incarnation of evil and is among the most evil men to live in all of time.

All of this leads to an important question.

In what kind of culture did Nazism grow?

Maybe you already know. Germany, during the Nazi era, was, by far, a Christian nation. People attended church on Sunday, there were thousands of pastors, and the vast majority of religious people in the nation would identify themselves as Christians.

Yet Bonhoeffer made a chilling observation about the kind of Christianity pervasive in Germany in the era of Hitler, World War II, and Nazism. The prevalent cultural theology was that of *cheap grace.*

It was within this laboratory that some of history's greatest atrocities were allowed to grow unchecked, even on the doorsteps of the Christian church. In its most exaggerated form, the idea and practice of cheap grace made the church incapable of fulfilling its role as the moral governor of society. It made the church irrelevant. The church was, in effect, sleeping while Hitler awakened the nation and led it to spread hatred around the globe.

Cheap grace made the church feel religious even while it was dying, and it made the church a less-than-innocent bystander while the world marched to war.

Cheap grace was false theology that—literally—led to unnecessary death.

GRACE COSTS SOMETHING

We must always be cautious about the cheapening of grace.

Grace might "let someone off," but it doesn't always let that person off easy. Sometimes God, who forgives us liberally, will force us to face the consequences of our actions. This doesn't mean that God is being less kind. In fact, it means that God cares enough to make us face what's hurting, or even destroying, us. Grace always costs something.

This is why Bonhoeffer used the term "costly grace" in contrast with "cheap grace." Of it, he said,

> Such grace is *costly* because it calls us to follow, and it is *grace* because it calls us to follow *Jesus Christ*. It is costly because it costs a man his life, and it is grace because it gives a man the only true life. It is costly because it condemns sin, and grace because it justifies the sinner. Above all, it is *costly* because it cost God the life of his Son: "ye were bought with a price," and what has cost God much cannot be cheap for us. . . .
>
> Costly grace confronts us as a gracious call to follow Jesus, it comes as a word of forgiveness to the broken spirit and the contrite heart.[2]

Bonhoeffer was saying that what cost Jesus everything ought to cost us something, and certainly it should never be taken for granted. Grace is free, but it isn't cheap.

As C. S. Lewis wrote of Aslan, he is not a "tame lion." He is *good*—but he is still a lion.

Grace is free, but it's also God's. Sometimes it is tough,

sometimes it is easy, but it is never cheap. Every time we extend grace to someone, it is an act of worship to God. We are being Christ to others.

So why have I included *this* chapter in the section of this book about *giving* grace? What is my point?

My point is that the kind of grace the world needs, and the kind of grace Jesus gives, is the kind of grace that will cost us something. It's the tough grace that causes us to chance losing a friend because we finally tell her what she needs to hear. It's the kind of grace that causes you to put yourself in great personal danger to stand up for the disenfranchised or enslaved. It's the kind of grace that might make people think you're weak, when you're actually strong—the kind of grace that will be misunderstood in a world that looks out for number one.

This book isn't imagining millions of Christians suddenly doing random acts of kindness. This book imagines what could happen when millions of Christians start to live the lifestyle of grace that inevitably costs them something, maybe something they don't want to give.

Sometimes it's our responsibility to tell people what they need to hear over what they want to hear, to treat them how they need to be treated as opposed to how they want to be treated, and to do for them what is best over what is easiest.

Grace can be hard and uncomfortable, and sometimes grace can earn us the hatred of those we love the most.

When a child is playing in the street, grace doesn't let him do whatever he wants. Grace intervenes.

Grace stands up for truth when people don't want to hear it, and grace stands in the gap for those who haven't a voice. Grace takes the hit. Grace decides to charge injustice from the front lines. Grace sometimes says what no one wants to hear and then keeps saying it until everyone has heard it.

We all come to uncomfortable moments in our lives when we have to confront people we love with the kind of grace that stings, or when we have to step out of our comfort zones to respond to a need. We have a tendency to delay these encounters as long as possible. We forget that love is patient and kind, that it trusts and hopes, that it is selfless and humble, and that it *protects*.

Protection isn't always invited or even welcomed, but it is often needed.

Tough grace is willing to protect those who cannot protect themselves. It fights for those who can't fight for themselves, and it steps into the fray even when there is a good chance of pain or discomfort.

What if a billion Christians began to live a lifestyle of grace as wildly as Jesus did? What if we cared enough about others to say and do what we know needs to be said and done, whether it's popular or not? How would the world be different if we were known for our grace—not the cheap kind, but the often costly kind—the kind that changes the world?

FOURTEEN

CRACKING PANDORA'S BOX

My sister didn't just *think* I was evil. She told me I was, and she was probably right.

When we were children, I took full advantage of every opportunity to make her life miserable. I would play tricks on her, embarrass her in front of her friends, and persuade my parents that she was treating me badly. Once I even convinced her to eat dog food.

My most evil trick occurred a few days after a tiny earthquake had shaken up the little town we were living in. The earthquake was almost unnoticeable, but in a town as small as ours, far from any earthquake-prone areas, it was big news. The next day, the front page of the local newspaper warned everyone about the massive, formerly dormant fault line that we were perched upon, the local schools had emergency drills requiring everyone to climb underneath their desks with their hands over their head, and every little gossip nook in the city was abuzz about the coming "big one."

My sister was the paranoid type, and I decided that this afforded me a prime opportunity to demonstrate to her who was actually in charge.

Unbeknownst to her, our grandma had given me a toy siren for Christmas. Up till now, I had never found a use for it. It sat in the bottom of some drawer awaiting the day my cunning little mind conjured up some mischief.

This was the day.

Julie was in the shower when I walked up to the bathroom door, sat the siren on the floor, and turned it on high. It rang at an ear-piercing level as I screamed at the top of my lungs, *"Julie, it's an earthquake, it's an earthquake! We're going to die! This is the big one! Run! Run!"*

Julie began screaming. I was still screaming. The dog was barking, the siren was blasting, and the world was surely falling apart.

Julie flung open the bathroom door, only to find me standing there laughing hysterically. She was not amused. Then she noticed the yellow plastic siren on the floor. Her mind quickly calculated the distance between it and my head. She picked it up, cranked her arm back, and flung it at warp speed.

CRACK!

"You're evil!" she screamed as my little siren, still blaring, bounced from my head to the wall to the floor. That was the first and last time I ever received a black eye from a girl. It was not the last time my sister called me *evil*.

———

As kids, we threw around that word *evil* thoughtlessly all the time. My prank was *evil* according to Julie, and I thought it was evil when she chose violence over a sense of humor.

The second-grade teacher whom everyone feared in my

school was evil, and all the cartoon characters and television personalities that foiled the plans of the good guys were evil. Marilyn Manson was evil, and so was the youth pastor in my church when he told the entire youth camp of my latest middle-school crush.

We used *evil* the same way we used certain words to describe food we didn't like and things we didn't like to do.

In other words, it was virtually meaningless.

THE ENTRANCE OF EVIL

The Ancient Greeks taught that Pandora was the first woman, and while she'd been endowed with every gift, including beauty, music, and persuasion, she was chiefly curious, and it was Pandora's curiosity that ushered evil into the world.

The chief of the gods, Zeus, decided that mankind needed to learn that disobeying the gods wasn't in their best interest. So, he devised a way to use the curious Pandora to send a resounding message to Earth's inhabitants that disobedience would result in inevitable suffering.

Zeus first collected all the world's maladies, illnesses, hardships, and pains. He piled them all into a little box that he gave to the curious Pandora to guard. Zeus chose Pandora because of her innocence. He knew she wouldn't devise a way to use the evils she possessed maliciously. But he also knew that her curiosity would eventually compel her to peek inside and unleash evil into the world.

That fatal peek would cause the world to change forever.

And peek she did, and the fabric of the world tore as Pandora, in her terror, watched the evil spirits rush uncontrollably from the box. She frantically tried to close the lid, but the force of their exit was too great. Finally she was able to smash the lid down, but it was too late.

She knew it. And the world has known it ever since. Evil has left the building, and in her split second of curiosity she had turned the fateful page of history. She had bitten the apple. She had unleashed something that couldn't be confined again.

DON'T PUT IT BACK IN THE BOX

Whether it's the historical account of Eve in Eden sneaking a bite of the apple, or the myth of Pandora's curious mistake, there is one overarching conclusion in these and a million other such stories: *evil is real, it is horrible, and it's at work.*

Evil has been unleashed. Every culture has its story of how it happened, but no one denies it exists.

It is free to make a mess of things, it has been up to its ruckus for a long time now, and we all know the results of it firsthand. We can point to heaps of broken promises and countless stories of the defilement of the image of God: raped women, murdered husbands, and poverty, pain, and disease. Evil has stained the purity of the human experience with deep, hopeless blackness, and evil's shadow has been cast over the best and the worst among us. Evil makes children orphans; it makes families fracture. Evil prompts greed to defraud innocent people of the fruit of their life's work.

Yet, despite our universal acquaintance with the work of evil, we have a deep-rooted propensity to dilute it, in our popular culture, of its horror and to treat it like child's play. We think we can handle it without being burned. We envision the worst examples of evil—the Hitlers, the Osama bin Ladens, the Pol Pots—and then reassure ourselves that our little white lies, even our hatred and our bitterness, could never ever make us *like that*.

We want the best of both worlds, and we think we can have it. While we may concede that Charles Manson or Adolf Hitler behaved evilly, we wouldn't dare characterize our selfishness that way, nor our arrogance nor our manipulation nor our anger nor our desire to climb the ladder at all costs. These behaviors aren't *evil*—they're just *bad* or maybe *dangerous*, but they're not evil. Selfishness isn't evil—it's just selfishness, right?

The Bible characterizes our minor indiscretions differently. We sometimes forget that there were far more petty little sins than earth-shaking big ones in the potent brew of iniquities that Jesus guzzled down on the cross.

Far more of us fall prey to these "white-collar" sins than to their more grotesque bigger brothers. For every murderer, for every fraud, for every serial liar, there are millions nursing envy, bitterness, pent-up anger, and hatred. One of the greatest lies we've been taught to believe is that these wrongs are *less wrong*.

Jesus taught us that nursing anger in one's heart is just as bad as murder, and that a glancing look of lust is the equivalent of adultery. He amped up the classification of our white-collar sins: they are capital crimes that deserve the death penalty.

He wasn't diminishing the significance of murder or adultery —he was elevating the significance of anger and lust. And he didn't do this to pile on the guilt either. He simply wanted to demonstrate to us that we're worse off than we think we are—so that we realize we need God more than we think we do.

God didn't carve the law in stone tablets just to institute a cosmic game of justice. God carved the law into stone tablets because he knew we needed a mirror turned toward us, to show us what's really inside. The purpose of the law was to demonstrate to us our need for God.

Our sin problem is like an iceberg. What peeks out over the surface is just a hint of what lies hidden. And when that hidden mountain of sin causes us to miss the mark, we're missing our chance to change the world. We're closing the tap of grace that's meant to flow freely from our lives into the lives of those we know and those we meet.

Our little evils leave us graceless in a world we're supposed to introduce to grace—to Jesus.

WITNESSING EVIL

Not long ago a young woman stumbled into the coffee shop in which I'm working this morning. It's about eight thirty right now. The sun is just finally getting fully out of bed, and the spirit of the morning is just now getting into full swing. The girl is no older than twenty-one. She's clearly high, perhaps an addict, and she's not hung over from last night—she's high *right now*.

I've been watching her for a while. She keeps trying to stand, trying to stay awake, trying to make sense of the world she's living in, but judging by the confusion on her face, she's not succeeding. It's as though she doesn't have a clue where she is.

Just a moment ago, she woke up swatting the air as if she were in a fight or under attack. Before that, she looked off curiously into the distance for at least twenty minutes. She seems to be mixing reality with whatever drug-induced confusion her mind is in.

She asked for a glass of water, perhaps hoping that she could wash this all away. They gave it to her, but she forgot about it. It's sitting there on the table in front of her, and she hasn't drunk a sip.

Here she goes again. She just stood . . . she almost fell . . . and now she's leaving.

I'm watching her walk down the sidewalk now.

Her arms are flailing oddly in the air like Jack Sparrow in *Pirates of the Caribbean*. Only this is real for her, and nobody's laughing. She seems totally lost and alone.

She has something evil flowing through her veins. *She* isn't evil—she may very well be a kindhearted, thoughtful, gentle girl, but the evil of drug abuse has taken her future by the neck and now threatens to squeeze the life out of it.

There she goes, off to somewhere and nowhere, and who knows when she'll come to, and who knows whether she'll even know where she is.

Her life is broken. Hope may seem impossibly far away, and in her isolation the chords of her life keep playing out of key, looking for the missing tone to bring harmony to the clanking and banging and questioning going on in her mind.

I've seen the remnants of some of the worst evil in the world. I wrote of some of it in my previous book, *Honestly*. I've seen broken hearts and broken lives. I've been the victim of some of it myself. The evil that makes poverty and pain, divorce and adultery, robbery and deception, war and vengeance, guilt and bitterness, paints our life stories in various shades of sorrow.

It was hard to listen to genocide victims describe their experiences, and it was hard to watch adorable but undernourished, sickly, and poorly clad children scavenging in the trash for their meal of the day. It's hard to see a brilliant teenager who has everything he needs to be anyone he wants to be in the world—except opportunity.

Occasionally, we should try our hardest to look past the exterior shell of the people we pass on the sidewalks and sit next to in cafés. We should look deeper than the manicured façade of those we criticize, those we dislike, and those who seem to struggle to make sense of their lives. Instead, we should ask what's in them that's *causing* them to drink the liquor of the enemy—and what elixir we might deliver to their sickened souls.

We have all sipped from that cup of evil. The Bible warns us that our hearts are *deceitfully wicked above all things*, and it pleads with us to arrest those demons that attempt to run amok in our own lives. In my family history we've seen the demonic work of alcoholism and infidelity and bitterness, anger, deception, manipulation, and theft firsthand. Sometimes I wonder why I'm not more scared of these dormant characteristics in my own DNA from the history of my family.

If I knew that a dangerous gang lived down the street from me, I would live very watchfully. I would install an alarm and add extra locks. I'd buy a weapon, call the police anytime I heard an unusual noise, and live vigilantly and cautiously, always aware of the danger lurking at my doorstep.

Why am I any less concerned about the evil that has stalked my family for generations? And I'm not alone—we all live with our own gangs lurking at our doorsteps. Let's call them what they are—*evil*. We have to fight them bare-knuckled to make sure they don't get the best of us. And we also have to fight on behalf of others who don't have the strength or wherewithal to fight for themselves.

It's evil when ambition causes men to work too hard to the neglect of their families. It's evil when deficient self-esteem causes a young lady to give herself to every boy who gives her any attention because she's so unsatisfied with how she looks. It's evil when selfishness causes a person with everything he needs in life to walk right past a friend or a loved one lying bloodied on the side of the road, beaten by life's misfortune. It's evil when pragmatism causes a businessman to tweak the system to his advantage and at the expense of the honest customers trusting him with their finances and future. It's evil when arrogance causes a human being to look down on another human being when it was only fate that allowed him to be born with opportunity when others arrived with misfortune.

I'm not saying that the people who fall prey to such common improprieties are evil. But it's time we start viewing our "little" maladies and misbehaviors and cut corners as the serious problems they actually are.

It was actually Jesus' brother—a skeptic turned bishop of Jerusalem—who taught, *If you've broken one part of the law you're guilty of breaking all of it.*[1]

What a profound idea. Profound in that it simultaneously lifts up life's little evils to their proper place while also freeing us of the weight of our most grandiose ones. James taught that *arrogance* is as evil as *murder*, but if you're a terrorist—as the apostle Paul once was—you are no more of a sinner than a liar. While sin's consequences cause different degrees of pain, God doesn't say, "That guy's a murderer, and that guy's only a liar."

God says, "Those guys are lawbreakers, and they must repent if they're going to be free to pursue a relationship with me."

What might happen if we started to think of our petty

selfishness with the same disdain we feel about Bernard Madoff's Ponzi scheme or the latest suicide bomber?

We might admit how broken we are and how much we need God.

———

If you're an alcoholic, they tell me, the first step to liberation is admitting you're an addict. You confess that you're sicker than you thought you were and that you've been deceiving yourself even more than you've been deceiving others. The same trigger that this confession pulls in the heart of an alcoholic is the trigger that repentance pulls in our hearts for every kind of evil.

What's glorious is that Jesus is a specialist at picking up evil by the nape of its neck and flinging it as far away as the east is from the west. Once we admit our need for him, he takes our evil and buries it at the bottom of the ocean. He helps us become free.

The apostle Paul knew evil well, and he knew firsthand God's power to rid a person of it. He had once been a Jewish theologian who knew everything he needed to know to recognize the Messiah, but instead he became a Christian-killer. He purposely, tactfully, and aggressively sought out followers of Jesus Christ and had them imprisoned or even murdered. He hunted all those who loved Jesus. He was a Bin Laden.

Then while journeying toward Syria, with letters in his hand authorizing the murder of even more Christians, Jesus appeared to him, blinded him, and reminded him of who was actually in charge.

Paul realized his sin in that moment, and he repented.

I recently read again one of Paul's less-familiar accounts

of this moment. He was writing to a church in modern Turkey when he reminded them,

> I want you to know, brothers and sisters, that the gospel I preached is not of human origin. I did not receive it from any man, nor was I taught it; rather, I received it by revelation from Jesus Christ. For you have heard of my previous way of life in Judaism, how intensely I persecuted the church of God and tried to destroy it.[2]

And *intensely* was a great word to describe it.

Paul was so feared by the earliest members of the Christian church that even after his conversion, it took some time before the early believers believed that he wasn't secretly a spy. Luke, the doctor, historian, and author of the books of Luke and Acts, wrote of the early church, "When he [Paul] came to Jerusalem, he tried to join the disciples, but they were all afraid of him, not believing that he really was a disciple."[3]

Eventually, the Bible says, a disciple named Barnabas believed that God even had the power to save a man like Paul. He trusted that Paul had actually converted, and he convinced the members of the Christian church to take him in and accept the man whom they would come to know as Christianity's greatest missionary.

For the rest of his life, Paul taught a gospel of transformation that could change the most evil heart because he was himself an eyewitness of it.

Recipients of great grace believe that God can do anything, even resurrect the darkest heart in the most difficult place.

Evil is real, but evil is incinerated when it collides with grace—through Jesus.

FIFTEEN

A GRACE-STARVED PLANET

THERE WAS A DAY LAST WEEK THAT I THOUGHT was particularly bad. All I did was complain and fuss, and nothing worked out well for me. I had problems with people and problems with circumstances. It seemed as if I were swimming upstream, and every little thing was a big thing. The wheels had come off my life somehow, and they didn't slowly ease off either. They went flying off—all in one fell swoop.

You know that feeling, right? Everything is going just fine. Life is moving on at a nice pace, blessings on every side, and peace seems to be watching over you. Then, suddenly, kaboom! Something goes south, and it pulls everything else in its wake. It's like a tidal wave, determined to disrupt any sense of equilibrium you might have enjoyed. Your own personal Katrina shows up unannounced.

Crises don't RSVP. They're like distant relatives who knock on your door to announce they're bunking with you for a little while.

In moments like these, you're tempted to look up at heaven, point at where you think God might be, and cry, "For goodness' sake, God! Give me a break."

In reality, I'm not sure these circumstances have anything to do with God. They probably have more to do with us. We have a tendency to make a mess of our lives pretty well without God's help. As I wrote in *Honestly*, being a Christian doesn't entitle you to a peace treaty with life. The ups and downs and twists and turns will roll on through, and somehow you've got to learn how to manage them.

Since that particular bad day, I flew to Africa—and there I ran headfirst into an attitude adjustment. It's amazing how self-absorbed we can become when life isn't going exactly as we want it to. Meanwhile, half the world is barely alive, and we're fussing because our quality of life is one step below luxury, by the standards of most of the world.

After spending half a week speaking across the major cities in South Africa, I am writing this in Kenya. The aid organization I support, World Help, is working with Liberty University on a project to reach hundreds of thousands of refugees fleeing for their lives from the encroachment of the worst famine to hit the Horn of Africa in sixty years.

One lady I just met had walked ten days with her six nearly starved children to get to a better place to raise her family after Islamic extremists in Mogadishu murdered her husband.

Now, that's a bad situation. But you know what? It got worse.

See, the *better* place she fled to was the sprawling refugee camp called Dadaab that sits an hour's drive into Kenya from the precarious border it shares with Somalia. When I landed in Dadaab, all I could see from the windows of the chartered plane were thousands of sprawling tents and ramshackle huts constructed for the refugees who had arrived by the thousands. In the last few months more than thirty thousand children have died here, and now nearly half a million refugees are living in camps that were originally designed twenty years ago to hold no more than ninety thousand people.

The seemingly unending conflict in Somalia and two years of searing sun with no respite of rain has formed a putrid brew of death and disease and hopelessness. The ground is cracked and the fields are lifeless, widows are forced to stretch a meal enough for one across families of five or six, and everyone is uncertain about their future.

People here would have long died if it weren't for the generosity of governments and NGOs and people of faith all over the world who've decided to help. It takes about $6,000 to deliver 240,000 meals to the folks living here.[1] At this moment, Liberty and World Help have four containers, with a total of more than 1,000,000 meals, en route to the port in Kenya. The food will be trucked here and will be distributed to these desperate people.

A million meals sounds impressive until you take into consideration that a million meals will provide one meal a day for each refugee for only two days. More has to be done. These people need grace, and they're not the exception. This world is broken in a billion different ways. It's bubbling over with desperate people, and we, as the followers of the God of grace, have been given the responsibility of spreading the goodness of God across the planet. We are to follow Jesus into this messy world, and let grace heal it through our kindness.

GIVEN GRACE, GIVE GRACE

Actually, it seems as though the world is erupting in suffering. Take, for instance, the issue of human trafficking. Each year six hundred thousand to eight hundred thousand children, women, and men are trafficked across international borders. Eighty percent of those are female and fifty percent are minors. There are at least two million trafficked children. The market value of "illicit human trafficking" is $32 billion a year. Sex trafficking is the "engine" of the global AIDS epidemic.

Sex trafficking is just one of the issues taking advantage of the most vulnerable people on our planet. Did you know that there are more slaves in the world today than at any time in history? At least 40 percent of all modern slaves are children, and 40 percent of the world's countries have not "registered a single conviction against perpetrators of trafficking and slavery."[2] Can you believe that in the modern world we are still dealing with the issue of humans enslaving other humans? It may be unconscionable, but it is still a reality. That has to change.

Then there is the fundamental issue of just having enough food. I just watched a video of my dear friend Dr. Vernon Brewer (president of World Help) standing in front of the shallow graves of children who had starved to death because of famine.

In this modern, advanced, technological, and wealthy world, there are still almost one billion people who struggle with hunger on a daily basis. That's more than the entire populations of North and South America, combined. Thirty percent of the people in sub-Saharan Africa are hungry. Two-thirds of the world's hungry people live in Bangladesh, China, the Democratic Republic of the Congo, Ethiopia, India, Indonesia, and Pakistan. The world's poor families spend 75 percent of their income on food, and the world's children are those most affected. In fact, one in four children does not get the nutrition they need, and every fifteen seconds a child dies of hunger.[3]

When someone rattles off such startling statistics as these, the college students I work with basically have a couple of deep-seated reactions. First, they don't get it. These are just numbers flying at their already media-saturated brains. *Millions* are the same as *thousands* or *billions*—either way, you just can't get your head around such big numbers. The second normal reaction is low-grade anger. They ask why someone, especially God, doesn't do something about all of this.

I think the answer to the first issue is to expose people to poverty firsthand, or at least train them to think about these figures differently and in more relevant ways. For instance, my friends at Cause Life tell me that one billion people lack access to clean water, more than six thousand children die every day because of it, and in Africa alone, more than forty billion hours are wasted each year by people having to fetch water from faraway sources.

Just more astronomical numbers, right?

But imagine what it would be like if your own best source of water was five miles away, a round-trip you made at least once a day, *every* day—and that source of water was a putrid pond of sewage that was filled with feces and urine.

Now imagine that your adorable eight-year-old niece had to fetch this water, and this was the water she drank, the water her mom used to cook her food. It's the water she would splash on her face on a hot day—and the water that caused her to live every single day of her life with dehydrating diarrhea. Like a pinhole in your oil tank, where the oil drips drop by drop out of your car, eventually, and with excruciating slowness, that little niece you love will be robbed of her chance at life because of one thing: bad water.

That's reality for thousands of children around the world.

When you think about slavery or sex trafficking in these terms, it causes your stomach to turn over, and in the heart of someone motivated by grace, it should produce a compelling drive to do something about it.

Imagine, for instance, that same adorable eight-year-old niece went with her parents for a summer trip through Europe's most glorious cities. She's having the time of her life looking at the Duomo in the heart of Italy's Renaissance city of Florence. She and her parents are looking straight up at the stunning architecture, observing the size and curvature of the building, the ancient decoration inscribed on its exterior, and how the folksy, old-world piazza hems the Duomo in. They feel that they've moved back in time to a simpler, more mythical era.

Just then her parents look down. Their daughter is nowhere in sight. They immediately snap into panic mode. Their pulses race, their eyes dart frantically in every direction, they call out her name, and then they scream it.

"Where are you? Where are you?"

By the time they're done frantically searching the growing crowd, after they have called upon the help of the local authorities, they suspect that their precious daughter is already in another place. What they don't know is that she's already in another city altogether, kidnapped by horrible people who intend to sell her to the highest bidder so he can act out his most satanic fantasies.

Imagine that that had been *your* fate, or the fate of your wife or sister or mother or best friend or the person you're closest to. How would that make you feel? Does it not cause you to shudder?

We tend to shut out this kind of suffering, deny it, or put it out of our minds because there's nothing we can do about it, so we might as well not even think about it. These scenarios are definitely downers, it's true—but nevertheless, they ought to make our blood boil and our eyes tear up.

We should be more affected than we are by these things. And when we reach the appropriate level of outrage, we'll actually do something about it—we'll stand in the gap for those who need us the most, and get our hands dirty the way Jesus dirtied his hands for us.

THE SECOND QUESTION

But what of that second typical response to these issues of human suffering? How do we deal with our tendency to accuse God of negligence when the world is in such dire shape?

Actually, I think when we look at the sky and ask God to do something, he says back to us, "I *am* doing something. I'm burdening *your* heart with this need. I'm allowing your life to collide with this crisis, and I'm giving you this burden for one reason—so that you can be my hands and feet to do something about it."

I believe with all of my heart that we are often the answers to our own burdens. The causes that make us cry and work and complain and plead and raise money and raise awareness and take red-eyes to other countries and sleep in huts and risk disease and danger are the same causes that God has assigned to us. They have become our responsibility—and it's our call, our turn, to make the difference that we're expecting and hoping others will make.

Compassion means action. It's not enough to just be moved by the fact that people are dying for the absolutely unnecessary reason of lack of food. It's not enough to cry over the terrifying plight of child prostitution or forced labor. It's not enough to look at the guy beaten on the side of the road and feel sorry for him.

We have to do something about it. True compassion means that we care enough to effect change. When the Bible says Jesus was "moved with compassion,"[4] the word *compassion* in biblical Greek implies a movement from the inside out. You are physically pained by what you see, and you almost *have* to do something to change it.

We are the answers to the problems we're most concerned about.

This isn't simply a matter of our emotional reaction to the world's people who are enduring all kinds of unjust suffering. For followers of Jesus Christ, our responses to these needs are of great theological significance.

Take, for instance, the time the self-righteous Pharisees asked Jesus to name for them the greatest commandment.

First, he rattled off the correct answer. He quoted the *shema* from the Old Testament, which compelled them to love God with all their hearts, souls, minds, and strength. That was the correct answer. But then Jesus volunteered an answer to a question they hadn't asked. He said, "And the second is like it: 'Love your neighbor as yourself.'"[5]

Jesus was just as interested about our concern and care for one another as he was about our concern and care for the Father. Our faith is a *lived-out* faith that demands the abundant distribution of love and grace to *others*.

Jesus talked about this all the time. And in fact, he talked of our acts of compassion as ways in which we worship God. Jesus said:

"For I was hungry and you gave me something to eat, I was thirsty and you gave me something to drink, I was a stranger and you invited me in, I needed clothes and you clothed me, I was sick and you looked after me, I was in prison and you came to visit me."

Then the righteous will answer him, "Lord, when did we see you hungry and feed you, or thirsty and give you something to drink? When did we see you a stranger and invite you in, or needing clothes and clothe you? When did we see you sick or in prison and go to visit you?"

The King will reply, "Truly I tell you, whatever you did for one of the least of these brothers and sisters of mine, you did for me."[6]

Once, I traveled to India with a couple of dozen students from Liberty University. We spent our days, from dawn to dusk, playing with orphans at one of the largest orphanages in the world. Those kids wore us weary with their games and laughter and barefoot soccer and hugs and songs and kindness.

One of the students on the trip came up to me to ask me when we were going to get to "doing some ministry," since we'd traveled all the way around the world to help these kids. I told him that we *were* doing ministry. What we call "playing," Jesus calls "worship" because he said that what we have done for one of the least of these has really been for him. We had given these kids the gospel, telling them the message of Jesus Christ—but now we were *showing* them the gospel by giving them our love. Our acts of compassion toward others are, in actuality, offerings of worship to God.

He should be worshipped more.

SIXTEEN

GRACE IN THE TRENCHES

THE SIREN WAS STILL WHISTLING AS I LUGGED my bags out of the train car. Like everywhere else in India, this town was crowded, hot, and an explosion of sights and sounds— and smells. It was pandemonium. That's what I love about India, and what drives me mad about it too. India is—above all things— an assault on your senses.

I had no idea that, in the middle of the chaos, I was moments away from my first personal encounter with abject poverty. That encounter still influences my life in a profound way.

It took place just as I exited the train station.

A shoeless child, with matted hair and dirt-stained clothes, stopped me dead in my tracks. He was adorable, with piercing eyes, pep in his step, and a certain likability that you feel between you and a child who wants to be your friend, your *little buddy*.

This little boy appeared to have, like most of India's street children, no home, no parents, no food, and no future. He was desperate with a kind of desperation that nearly no one I know has ever experienced. When I met him I had, for sure, more "stuff" on my person than this little boy would own in his entire life.

Meanwhile, a car was waiting to rush me off to the old British mansion-turned-hotel where I was to stay for a few days. People were yelling at me from every direction to move on, and my hosts were begging for the opportunity to just get me out of there to my peaceful enclave.

All I could do was stare at that little boy—and wonder, just for a minute, what it would be like if I were him.

In that momentary juncture of generosity and urgency, I faced a choice between my own interests and the grace that I believe, and that I teach, should be emblematic of compassionate followers of Jesus.

It would take only a few seconds to show that child some kindness, as I would hope someone would do for me. Or I could politely slide into the car and take off to my refuge from the suffering around me.

I am sad to say that I closed my eyes and covered my ears. I walked to the other side of the curb, climbed into the car, and chose to let that little guy fend for himself.

I didn't play the part of the good Samaritan. Instead, I was like the priest who walked by—too preoccupied, too busy, too pressured, too religious, and too uncaring.

For weeks, the image of that little boy stayed imprinted on the forefront of my mind. It's still there. It has formed a scar on my heart that will ensure that I never forget what happened on that rowdy train platform in India.

This singular experience somehow birthed the compassion in my heart to bring Jesus' grace to the world. Jesus, for sure, wouldn't have walked past that little boy.

Oddly enough, my own refusal to help change that Indian child's destiny has changed my own.

I only wish I knew his name.[1]

JESUS SAVED US TO SERVE,
NOT TO BE SERVED

Jesus would have known that child's name. He wasn't too busy being God to care about the hurting. He was focused, almost entirely, on others from the very beginning. His disciples, on the other hand, struggled, as we do, to embrace grace over self-interest.

Up until a certain point, Jesus' disciples actually thought that they were going to follow Jesus on his white horse right into Jerusalem as he established his kingdom and made the world his servant. But Jesus wasn't interested in having the world serve him. He came to serve the world. His disciples' dreams of grandeur would soon collide with the reality that their path to stardom was more like a pending collision with the rich and the powerful of Rome *and* Jerusalem.

Jesus had fallen like a bunker buster into the religious milieu of his day, and the blast was strong enough to shake the most secure and powerful from their settled existence at the top of their ivory towers.

Jesus wasn't playing games.

And sometimes the good guys finish last.

See, his grace had an edge to it, a determination, and it couldn't be derailed by a bad day or a difficult season of life. His service was radical and principled, and he didn't care what the aristocracy thought of it. It wasn't the grace of teddy bears and water guns. It was the grace of boxing matches and horse breaking.

So Jesus did crazy things in order to serve the world. He went to places he shouldn't have gone. He said things he wasn't supposed to say. He spoke about topics that were off-limits and taboo, and he did it all within earshot of those whose entire reputations were based upon how awesome people thought they were—or perhaps on how awesome *they* saw *themselves* to be.

Jesus made fun of their self-aggrandizement, and in the face of their outraged power he served the world to salvation.

That had been his purpose from the beginning: to save and serve the world with or without them—and with or without his disciples, for that matter. He was going to do it selflessly, by grace.

Jesus was the selfless God who expected his occasionally highfalutin disciples to be in the trenches with him, and when they weren't, he was there anyway, demonstrating what they should be doing.

Take, for example, that awkward scene when his disciples had become too arrogant to wash one another's feet. Jesus didn't think twice about grabbing the towel himself. He had come to the earth for the towel. That's why he was here.

Jesus recruited fishermen because they were already used to having a little dirt on their hands. Jesus' followers were to be selfless, above all.

SELFLESSNESS MAY MEAN DEATH

Jesus eventually decided to amp everything up. He told the disciples that it would cost them something to follow him forward.

He laid it all out, with no room for misunderstanding. If his followers were traveling down this road in the hope of future fame or for a place at the right hand of Jesus or because Jesus provided a better career opportunity than anything else available to them, or if this was some self-centered way of persuading God to bless them, or if this was just part of their culture, then they should know that this *game* was about to become deathly serious.

Jesus came to serve the world, even if it meant death.

He told them in plain language that this could cost them their lives and, if not their lives, it would most certainly cost them something that they would rather not live without.

Jesus was right, by the way. Over the coming decades, his apostles and other disciples would be beaten, cursed at, homeless, despised, reviled, and persecuted in every sick fashion a psychopath could possibly imagine. In fact, all but one of the apostles would be martyred.

Matthew was killed by a sword in Ethiopia; Mark died after being dragged by horses through the streets in Alexandria, Egypt; Luke was hanged in Greece; Peter was crucified upside down; James the Just (half brother of Jesus) was clubbed to death in Jerusalem; James the son of Zebedee was beheaded by Herod Agrippa I in Jerusalem; Bartholomew was beaten to death in Turkey; Andrew was crucified on an X-shaped cross in Greece; Thomas was reportedly stabbed to death in India; Jude was killed with arrows; Matthias, successor to Judas, was stoned and then beheaded; Barnabas was stoned to death; Paul was beheaded under Nero in Rome.[2]

Grace is generous, but it isn't free. It will always cost you something when you decide to give—whether or not you receive anything in return.

SO THAT WE WILL GET DIRTY TOO

Jesus laid aside his life in the presence of God, donned the form of man, and came down to wallow in the mess that sin had made of the world, on the chance that man might learn to love God again.

I love how one author has put it:

> This is no run-of-the-mill messiah. His story was extraordinary. He called himself divine, yet allowed a minimum-wage Roman soldier to drive a nail into his wrist. He demanded purity, yet stood for the rights of a repentant whore. He called men to march, yet refused to allow them to call him King. He sent men into all the world, yet equipped them with only bended knees and memories of a resurrected carpenter.[3]

Jesus inaugurated a kind of faith the spirit of which is encapsulated in the words of the great missionary C. T. Studd: "Some wish to live within the sound / Of church or chapel bell, / I want to run a rescue shop / Within a yard of Hell."[4]

SELFISHNESS AND GRACE

Selfishness is the great vice that robs us of our ability to be gracious. It is the opposite of grace, and it is a defining characteristic of every horrible tyrant in history, every villain in literature, and every person who causes more harm than good in the world. Selfishness is the opposite of Jesus.

This selfishness is deeply rooted inside of us, and it's like a poison that robs us of our opportunity to change the world. It causes us to be hypocritical and ungrateful. It causes us to walk by hungry children living on train platforms in India.

Neither you nor I earned the good things God has given us. We didn't earn the forgiveness of our sins or the roofs over our heads or the jobs we enjoy or the parents who've taken care of us or the children who make us laugh.

God *gave* us these things. *He* actually owns them, and we have them on loan from him. We have received a dose of his grace, and we in turn should be full of grace for other people.

Even as I type these words, I'm particularly moved by the thought of children in Somalia who are making their beds tonight out of nothing but barren sand, their undernourished skin pulled like elastic over their brittle bones. In all likelihood, they will soon die.

It reminds me of the report I once listened to featuring a scholar who is an expert on lullabies from around the world. He studies the songs that mothers sing to woo their children to sleep from Europe and Asia, from the United States and South America. He ended his explanation by citing one sung by Somalian mothers to their children: "Go to sleep my child, and hunger will go away."

The most peaceful thing that this mother can say to woo her children to sleep is that sleep will make their hunger pangs go away.

I believe Jesus cares about that mother and her children, and the millions like them around the world. He also cares about those in spiritual darkness and modern-day slavery, and those who are sex-trafficked and abused and neglected.

Jesus is welcoming us to play a part in his plan to cover the earth with God's kindness. It's time we join him in the trenches.

God expects us to get our own hands dirty just as he dirtied his own. He wants to meet us—not in the sanctuary but in the slums. Where hopelessness resides is where the rivers of grace are meant to flow most freely.

God doesn't save us so that we can soak in religion but so that we can go out and spread his love to the masses.

God doesn't want us carefully confined behind our church walls in the euphoria of worship.

He wants us out in the world, determined to bring change to it.

He wants us to make history, to leave this a better world than we found it, and he wants his children to be known by his kindness.

God's not waiting for us at the altar. He's waiting for us to take the altar to the streets.

SEVENTEEN

HOW TO PERFORM MIRACLES

THIS JOURNEY TO RURAL INDIA HAD A SINGU-
lar purpose. I wanted to glean as much wisdom as I could from
one of the patriarchs of the Indian church.

The pastor I was visiting was now an old man, and his
body bore the bruises of incalculable beatings, more than a few
imprisonments, and too many threats to remember. He was a
modern Paul who had walked for miles down footpaths to plant
new churches. He had personally collected and cared for more
than ten thousand orphans, and he had pioneered churches in
every state in India. His ministry among lepers and orphans
had earned him an award from India's prime minister. He was
famous—mainly for the suffering he endured for Christ. His
Christianity was never accepted in his state in India, a bastion of
Hindu fundamentalism. When I visited him, he was just about
to experience one of the most serious threats his life and ministry had ever endured. You would expect him to be worried and
bitter, beaten down by life, and sorrowful. Instead, he was jovial;
he laughed incessantly with one of those deep and genuine types
of laughter that you cannot fake, and he never complained. He

was a man of grace—a man who loved Jesus, loved people, and would suffer anything if it meant the opportunity to tell another person about him.

When I visited him, he was an archbishop administering thousands of churches and hundreds of schools and still taking care of those ten thousand orphans. He was a spiritual leader to millions of people and handled millions of dollars, yet he lived in a single room connected to a small bathroom. He believed in austerity as a pilgrim of Christ on planet Earth, and he spent all of his time storing up treasures in heaven. He was a man who exuded faith. He lived like Jesus because he was so close to him that Jesus' values had become his own.

The archbishop often met Jesus in life's trenches ministering to orphans and victims of leprosy and AIDS. His hands were dirty, but his work had brought healing to the masses.

He agreed to my visiting him for a week, eating three times a day with him and having conversation after conversation about Jesus and the gospel and India and grace.

But it was a risky thing to spend a week with a hunted man. At any moment, the militants could arrive, beating their kettledrums, chanting their hatred, and singing in worship of their gods. I can see in my mind what it would be like when they caught up with us—it was like an Indiana Jones movie, just before the maniacs yank the heart out of your body with their bare hands.

So you can imagine the fear that washed over me when I was jarred from sleep one night to the sound of chanting and drumming in the distance. At first I was paralyzed with fear, but within seconds adrenaline pushed me into survival mode. I ran up two flights of stairs and scanned the horizon, looking for the approaching band of militants, but saw no one. I ran to the other side of the building, but they weren't there either.

So down the stairs I dashed. Cracking open the door, I slid out, fled to the corner, and peeked around it, expecting to find an approaching mob.

What I saw was a tuba.

Next came a horse bearing a turban-adorned man like a maharaja. Several people held a canopy over the man and the horse. Then came a trumpeter, and all kinds of people dancing and singing and cheering and rejoicing, going crazy, totally intoxicated with joy and celebration.

My saffron-adorned, flag-waving, idol-chanting mob was actually a family celebrating an Indian wedding. They weren't coming to kill the archbishop, or me—they were welcoming us into their party!

JESUS AT CANA

You'll remember that an Eastern wedding, like the one I witnessed in India, was the setting of Jesus' first miracle. Actually, not much has changed in two thousand years. There would have been the same revelry and music, the same canopy above the heads of the bride and groom in the processional, and for this one day those being wed in an Eastern tradition would have been treated like kings and queens—actually, for a week. There were some differences, of course (the Indians wore turbans and the Jews once wore crowns), but generally a modern Indian wedding in a rural area looks and feels much like a Jewish wedding thousands of years ago.

It's safe to say that Jesus would have been partying, dancing, singing, and having the time of his life when he decided to perform (in response to his mother's request) his inaugural miracle at a wedding in an obscure little village called Cana. Cana wasn't a bustling metropolis. It was probably home to only a few hundred people, and the occasional wedding would have been about the only thing of significance that happened there.

It's clear from the biblical story in John 2 that someone in the wedding party was somehow related to Mary or Joseph, Jesus' parents. That explains why Mary seemed responsible for organizing the wedding, and when the wine ran out she was the one who seemed to bear the burden. She rushed off to Jesus to notify him and to *compel* him to do something about it.

Jesus responded in an unusual way: "Woman, why do you involve me?" (John 2:4).

If I had ever called my momma from South Carolina *woman*, I would have been beaten to a pulp. I would not suggest calling *your* momma *woman* either unless, of course, you want to have a legitimate black eye to spice up your Halloween regalia. But in Jesus' time this wouldn't have had the same connotation as it does today. Odysseus referred to Penelope as *woman*, and Augustus called Cleopatra *woman*. If that had been an insult, Cleopatra would have had Augustus beheaded before the echoes died, but in Jesus' time it sort of meant *lady*. It was a term of endearment. When you read the whole passage, you get a better picture of Jesus' love for his momma.

Then he said something else: "My hour has not yet come" (v. 4).

Clearly, Jesus didn't want to meddle in wine making before he started making blind men see and dead men walk. In fact, there's a hint of frustration. He's saying, in essence, "But, Mom, that's not what this is for. It's not time. It's not why I'm here."

I love the earthiness, the humanity, of the story as Jesus and his mom banter back and forth, just as we've all done with our own parents.

And just as our own parents have done with us in those situations, Jesus' mom totally ignored him. She looked over at the servants and said, "Do whatever he tells you" (v. 5). It's as if she gave Jesus a wink—she wasn't taking no for an answer. Then she walked away with sass in her step.

Then Jesus did it.

Because even Jesus was scared of his momma.

The Bible says he ordered the servants to fill six massive jars to the brim with water. Each jar, typically used for ceremonial washing, could contain twenty to thirty gallons of water.

In the blink of an eye, the water transformed into wine. The text implies effortlessness, almost the tone of an afterthought. Jesus just did it. It wasn't hard, it didn't take much time, and there were no fireworks. He just quietly did something supernatural without drawing any attention to himself whatsoever.

The head chef of the banquet happened to walk by just after Jesus had meddled in history, and he tasted the wine. The Bible says he loved it! He declared in astonishment, "Everyone brings out the choice wine first and then the cheaper wine after the guests have had too much to drink; but you have saved the best till now!" (v. 10).

And we learn something about Jesus here—Jesus doesn't do anything halfheartedly. If he's going to make wine, it's going to be the best stuff *ever*.

BUT WHY DID HE DO IT?

But the most important question in this entire story is, *Why did Jesus do it here and why did Jesus do it now?*

There's a cultural reason, and a theological one. The cultural reason is that it would have been enormously shameful, in a culture that scorns shame above all things, for there to be inadequate provisions for a once-in-a-lifetime party like this. Weddings were enormous celebrations that were treated with an importance almost impossible for us to understand. Our culture has devalued marriage to a degree that you can fly through a Vegas drive-through and get a dress-up Elvis to certify your marriage. But back in Jesus' time, a wedding was the culmination of the lifework of the parents and the beginning of their legacy. It was also the most important moment in the lives of their children. It was a family affair, a celebration you waited your whole life for. It sometimes lasted for days, and it was the responsibility of the family to provide the food and drink to accompany the party. Not providing enough food and wine for the party would have been an almost unforgivable offense.

Chances are Joseph had passed away by now, since Mary seemed clearly responsible for the situation—more typically, this would have been the husband's responsibility. So, *culturally speaking*, Jesus' heart went out to his mom. This problem, which might seem insignificant to us, was to Mary an emergency.

Theologically speaking, I think Jesus was making a cataclysmic point about his values and his priorities. In the Bible, the purpose of Jesus' miracles is abundantly clear. John 2:11 says of this miracle, "Here in Cana of Galilee was the first of the signs through which he revealed his glory." Jesus performed miracles to display his glory.

Jesus was demonstrating what makes him unique, what makes him worth worship, what makes him worth our attention and our affection. He was displaying his glory.

Glory is a hard word to define, but you know it when you see it. When the sun sets in a display of indefinable color, or when you look at the life's work of an unparalleled artist, or when you stand staring so intensely at the ocean that you can see where it meets the sky on the horizon, you say, "That's glorious." *Glorious* implies that something is totally unique from everything else, worth admiration. It's a synonym for being in *awe* of something.

Now, weren't there plenty of other, maybe more effective, ways for Jesus to show his glory? Couldn't he have levitated in the center of Jerusalem or Rome and spoken truth with the voice of thunder? Couldn't he have used his finger to draw neon pictures across the Judean sky? Couldn't he have pulled a Jack Bauer on the Roman legions, turned the Roman emperor into a pillar of salt, or stripped the Pharisees to their skivvies in the middle of a crowded street?

Jesus could have caused everyone on planet Earth to say "Wow" in a million different ways.

Instead, he chose to perform his first "glory demonstration" in a humble village in a humble home, in order to keep the family he loved from being shamefully embarrassed.

It was like using a bazooka to kill a mosquito.

And it's just like Jesus to "waste" his grace on the everyday man. Jesus would rather be with his family, at his cousin's wedding, than making a scene in Rome. In fact, it's stunning that Jesus never traveled to Rome in his entire life and ministry. The trip would have been irrelevant to him—it would have been a distraction. He didn't need to go to the seat of power to change history. He could have done it from Nazareth if he'd wanted.

He would rather share his love with the willing few than fight to persuade the unwilling masses. Jesus, from the very beginning, came to planet Earth with a different set of values. Glory was to go where people least expected it and to love those who least deserved it.

That was glorious to Jesus.

GRACE GLORIES IN THE LITTLE THINGS

We're inclined to put grace and miracles in separate categories. One is supernatural and the other is a little more human, regular, less attractive. In actuality, there are no miracles without grace, and therefore grace is sort of a miracle in and of itself. It was God's grace that prompted Jesus to employ his power to make sure his family wasn't embarrassed and the party could go on. Likewise, it was God's grace that prompted Jesus to employ his power to raise Lazarus from the dead or to heal the lame man or the demonized man or the man with leprosy.

Grace is the miracle that each of us can exercise at will in the world around us. We can't cause seas to part, but we can drop cash-filled envelopes anonymously on the desks of single moms. We can't turn water into wine, but we can sacrifice a little bit of our income to pay for a well to be drilled in a slum in an impoverished village. We can't banish suffering, but we can make it more bearable for those navigating through one of life's difficult decisions.

Almost every admirable virtue begins with grace, and almost

every act of unmerited kindness begins there too. We are ourselves miracle workers, but the greatest miracles happen when we surprise the least deserving and the least expecting with kindness—overwhelming, superabundant, lavishly displayed *kindness.* When we do, the recipients of our kindness will often say, "God sent a miracle."

Grace, and the miracles that come from it, are both means of bringing glory to God. They testify to his goodness and his kindness in our own lives, and they demonstrate to the world that he is noble and he has come down in the trenches with us to bring us up to *glory.*

When the apostle Paul wrote, "Now then, we are ambassadors for Christ, as though God were pleading through us,"[1] I think he had both a message and a lifestyle in mind. Of course, he was compelling the Corinthian church to proclaim the gospel to people—to everyone, in fact. But he was also compelling them to *live the gospel of grace* in their daily lives. He was begging them to be both *recipients* of grace and *conduits* of grace, through which the kindness of God is dispersed to a broken and messy world.

———

A week with the archbishop convinced me of one thing: if he were Jesus, he would have wasted his time doing a miracle in a village wedding too. More often than I'd like to admit, I would be inclined to play to the crowd and make a big scene—and collect the fanfare.

The archbishop taught me that *real grace* has nothing to do with what you get out of it. *Real grace* has everything to do with what you put into it. Real grace involves giving so that others can get more of God's goodness in this often difficult life.

The archbishop is dead now.

His legacy lives on, because he left miracle after miracle in his wake. He poured grace into barren places and left weary hearts and impoverished people alive with *living water.*

There are orphans who are now doctors and professors and churches in places where the gospel had never been before. There are lepers who are smiling, widows who aren't worrying any longer, and men who are actually acting like men—loving God and their families as Christ loved the church.

These are the real miracles, the kind of miracles we need, and the kind of miracles you can perform in the lives of people every day. Grace calls us to turn the everyday into the miraculous.

Every act of kindness is a parting of someone's Red Sea.

EIGHTEEN

—

WHAT COULD HAPPEN IF GRACE COVERED THE EARTH

I BELIEVE WE ARE ON THE CUSP OF A REVOLU-
tion that will change the world, and this revolution will be a
grace revolution.

It will be marked by millions of followers of Jesus Christ
choosing to live lives marked by the generosity and kindness
that he modeled for us. We will fight for the oppressed and the
impoverished, we will say what needs to be said to bring hope
and help to those in need, and we will leave in our wake evidence that grace has changed our own lives—and that grace can
change others too.

We won't think small—not about what our lives filled with
grace can accomplish, and not about what could happen if the
church was born again in a new generation marked primarily
by her kindness and benevolence toward a world in need.

That's why I wrote this book.

I had a vision that we could do better than we've done. I
suspected that grace, which ought to be the most conspicuous of
Christian virtues, is too often the most difficult to find. I imagined for a moment what could happen if the church came alive

again in this area of her life—if we spoke with grace and gave with grace and fought with grace and exercised compassion with grace and loved God because of his grace. What if we gave grace to the undeserving? What if we let grace cause us to believe in the unlikely? What if our reputation as people of grace became so profound and so prominent that it overshadowed our mega-churches and megaministries, our political positions, and our rock-star personalities?

What if this generation of Jesus-followers decided to do everything in its power to live as Jesus lived?

It's a grand vision that begins to become reality when individuals like you and me decide to live with a little more grace in our lives day by day. The revolution begins when we sacrifice a little of our money to help those in need. It begins when we post on Facebook our concerns about the tragedy of modern-day slavery. It begins when we fight for those infected by AIDS and malaria. It begins when we choose to treat a colleague at work differently than he or she is treating us. It begins when we step out of our comfort zones and imagine what might happen if our lifestyle of grace made us to someone else what Jesus has been to the world.

It begins when we forgive the unforgivable, when we extend the same grace toward others that we hope they would have for us.

I believe, as I've written and spoken about in many different places and on many different occasions, that you're more important than you think you are. History may be reserving a special place on her stage for your crowning moment—but in the kingdom of God, let's not define a "crowning moment" as the moment when we're best known or most successful. Rather, it should be when we're able to make God's love most visible in the most difficult and unlikely places.

Your life could be like a falling domino that flips thousands more. Eventually, the repercussions of that one domino falling may cause mountains to fall into the sea, and the lame to walk, and the blind to see. Your life could become the essential stitch in a beautiful tapestry yet to be made. You could be the behind-the-scenes character who plays an indispensable part in the plot of the story.

I don't know for sure if you're more important in the story of grace than you think you are, but I don't want you to live as if you're not. I want you to live every day as if history is waiting on *you*. Jesus specializes in using the least likely people in historic ways. If you feel as though you're the least likely person to change the world, then you might be the very one he's been looking for. He still uses fishermen and tax collectors, and second-grade teachers and stay-at-home moms and businesspeople, to turn the dials of time.

I believe you're more important than you think you are because we're living in one of the most important moments in the history of the Christian church. This is why it's so important that we urgently begin to live lives of grace. The stakes are so high! In some places, there has never been more promising growth in Christianity, and in others there has never been a greater fight to preserve it. It seems that a massive reshuffling is taking place on the planet—religiously and politically, economically and generationally. God has granted us an amazing, and precarious, gift to be living today.

Millions of Muslims, Hindus, Buddhists, and Chinese atheists and animists are beginning to follow Jesus, and millions of

Jesus' followers are turning their eyes to the poor and oppressed. At the same time, more Christians have died as martyrs in recent years than in all of Christian history,[1] and the great, historic cities of Christian history have been flooded by secularism and an indifference toward Jesus.[2] The contrast between the explosive growth of Christianity in some parts of the world[3] and the war being waged to eradicate it in others makes it evident that something of great significance is happening in the times we're living in, and Jesus is at the heart of it. Jesus' grace is at work in empowering Christian martyrs to confess Christ while being stoned in Iran, and he is giving grace to the families of the Christians who were placed in shipping containers and dropped in the Eritrean desert to bake to death.[4] Jesus' grace is also moving among the exploding churches in South America and Africa as they send missionaries—by the thousands—to the most anti-Christian places in the world.

The church is on the move, and people everywhere are searching for something deeper, something meaningful, something that makes sense of this crazy world we're living in. Their souls are looking for God, and grace is the gravity that draws them there. Grace is the means by which the kingdom of God is seen on planet Earth.

With more than a billion Christians living today, grace should be plastered on the lives of Jesus' followers on every street corner and in every office building, on television and the Internet, and in a billion random acts of kindness that mark the values of men and women who deserved little from God—but have received much.

Sometimes it's hard to see the grace of Jesus in the suffering and pain of those whose lives are balanced on a knife's edge, in danger of falling at any time. Let us live so that grace shines brilliantly through us as we cut through the fog of suffering with God's kindness.

Poverty grips millions. Sex trafficking, human slavery, sexual abuse, and a lack of education are robbing whole generations of young people of their chance to change the world. Without grace, no one turns away from his own greed and selfish interest and toward those in need. Nor does anyone find Jesus without grace.

Now is the time for the followers of Jesus to scatter his grace to the ends of the world. It's time we take our place as the ones called to bring light and peace to God's planet, to demonstrate to the world that he's good. It's our responsibility and our opportunity to redesign the world in a way that makes God smile and makes this planet a little more like heaven.

Grace ought to make us better people, but it ought to also make this world a better place.

It starts with me, and it starts with you.

GET TO IT!

Phil Cooke wrote the other day on his blog that "goals are dreams with deadlines."[5]

His point was that it's not enough to simply want something to happen, or imagine the day when your dream becomes reality. You have to get to it. You have to rustle up the energy, make a plan, take the next achievable step, and continue to work the plan until what was once only a dream is real and touchable and a foundation for your next and greater dream.

Another friend of mine, Robert, gave me a great word of

advice a few months ago that I think Phil would agree with. He said, "If you have a big goal, then you have to ask yourself two questions every single day to make it reality: (1) What's most important? and (2) What's next?" If you just do that each day, Robert told me, then suddenly your wildest dream can become your daily experience, and one day at a time, you can make amazing things happen with the help of God.

I had a dream in my mind when the message of this book started to grow in my heart. In my last book, *Honestly*, I imagined what could happen if a billion Christians actually started to *live* what they *say they believe*. In *Dirty God* I'm imagining what could happen if a billion Christians began to scatter grace to the ends of the earth.

I'm imagining a generation of Christians who are kind and benevolent, generous and gracious, who strengthen others by simply coming into contact with them, and who turn the suffering world into a gentler, kinder place—a place where widows aren't alone, where orphans have homes, where the hungry are fed, where the diseased are healed, where wandering souls can find rest, and where the brokenness of this world is transformed by the grace of God through the people of God.

I'm imagining a world where Christians are known by the grace they've received from Jesus and the grace that they in turn have reinvested in the world because of him.

But let's be honest: the truth is that Christians, on most days and in most places, probably aren't known as people of grace, either within the church or outside it. We're often perceived as judgmental and holier-than-thou by a questioning world, and within the church we find ourselves sucked into the kind of backbiting and gossiping that's not befitting of people who genuinely care for one another. We often hold others to standards we don't hold ourselves to, and if faced with the opportunity to do something for ourselves or something for others, we're far too likely to look out for number one.

What's tragic is that our preoccupation with other things, and with ourselves, has robbed a world of the grace it desperately needs from Jesus through regular people like us. There's a particular role you must play in God's redemptive story, and that role is to be seasoned with grace.

I'll say it again: it's time to get to it.

There are thousands of kinds of brokenness and millions of broken people pleading for help.

God's solution is grace through *us*.

The answer to all the problems of the world is the awakening of the people of God to care enough about those problems to actually do something about them.

My friend Rick Warren believes this too. He believes that an activated church is the secret to addressing the major needs strangling the hope of billions on planet Earth.

What he calls the *five global giants* are the problems affecting *billions*, not millions, of people: spiritual emptiness, a lack of servant leadership, extreme poverty, pandemic diseases, and illiteracy.

Rick believes that the only institution significant enough to address these giants is the global church, and the means by which the church can address them is grace. The church is, Warren says, the largest distribution network in the world:

> There are more churches in the world than all the Wal-Marts, McDonalds and Starbucks combined. The church was global 200 years before anyone else thought of globalization. We

could take you to thousands of villages around the world where the only institution to speak of is the church.[6]

Warren believes that

there aren't enough doctors to solve all the issues in the world, there aren't enough teachers to solve all the issues in the world, and there aren't enough missionaries to solve all the issues in the world, but there is [an] army of believers sitting in churches waiting to be mobilized. . . . Ordinary people, empowered by God, making a difference together, wherever they are. . . . The greatest need of the twenty-first century is to release the pent-up, latent power of the average believer in churches local around the world. If we could figure out a way to turn an audience into an army, to turn consumers into contributors, to turn spectators into participators; it will change the world. It's time to stop debating and start doing. It's time for the church to be known for love, not for legalism; for what we're for, not for what we're against. It's time for the church to be the church.[7]

Pastor Rick has spent more than a decade teaching that the answer to the five global giants is for the global church to begin to aggressively engage in the five major things Jesus did in his ministry: plant churches, equip servant leaders, assist the poor, care for the sick, and educate the next generation.

All five of these ministries of Jesus were motivated by grace, on behalf of God, to people. And it all begins with grace, as the recipients of grace become distributors of grace to a world in desperate need of it.

Our compassion for the world begins with a vision of what

the world would be like if it were flooded with the grace of God through the people of God, but it mustn't end with *vision*, with a *dream*. That dream must be coupled with the get-it-done attitude that actually turns vision into history.

WE HAVE ALL THE HOPE IN THE WORLD

The English author Malcolm Muggeridge has written that "Jesus audaciously abolished death, transforming it from a door that slammed to, into one that opened to whoever knocked."[8] This truth provided Dietrich Bonhoeffer with the ultimate peace as he was being led away to his execution for being a lone voice against Hitler. Bonhoeffer believed that death was a "beginning and not an end." He wrote:

> From the resurrection of Christ . . . a new and purifying wind can blow through our present world. . . . If only a few people believed that and acted on it in their daily lives, a great deal would be changed.[9]

What was Bonhoeffer's point?

He believed that a little bit of human effort, coupled with the power of God, could change the world. His belief was cultivated in a truly faithless time, yet even in that faithless moment this truth was abundantly clear.

Even in the very pit of hell, Jesus could still change the hearts and destinies of men and women—even in the most unlikely places at the most unlikely times, and in the face of the most daunting challenges.

If Dietrich Bonheoffer, in Nazi Germany, could possess—and act on—this kind of faith in the practical life of costly grace, then what kind of faith should we have in our own day? The church is growing at record speed around the world. Christianity might *seem* to be waning in the West, but in actuality, there is as much progress as regress. The megachurch movement has, in the last twenty years, birthed the largest churches in Christian history. Missionary work around the world has made the completion of the Great Commission a conceivable reality in our lifetime, and in the most unlikely places in the world we have seen explosive church-planting movements birth millions of new believers.

These are days worthy of exceptional faith and hope because of the potential that surrounds us, but we must not become lackadaisical and complacent. We must do everything in our power to make the grace of the Lord Jesus Christ as prevalent as possible on planet Earth. Each of us has a part to play, and each of those roles is of supreme importance. Each of us has the power to spread within *our* world an extra layer of the grace of God.

We must not take this opportunity for granted. We should grab this chance so tightly our knuckles turn white.

THE STAKES ARE HIGH

A few years ago, I traveled to Tunisia with a group of Liberty University students to study modern Islamic life and practice.

Tunisia is a truly beautiful country, filled with enormously kind and hospitable people. We traveled from the top to the bottom of the nation. We visited the stunning ruins of one of the Roman Empire's largest coliseums, took a camel ride through the

Sahara desert, visited the set of Luke Skywalker's home from *Star Wars*, and even chartered a harrowing four-wheel-drive adventure over the towering sand dunes in the southern part of the nation. All the while, we taught the Liberty students about Islam; introduced them to local people, food, and customs; and even booked rooms in a hotel next to a mosque so the students could be jarred awake in the early morning by the sound of the call to prayer.

It was the trip of a lifetime.

What many of the students were surprised to learn was that this nearly entirely Islamic nation had once been a seat of early Christian thought. Tunisia was the home of the church father Augustine, and it was the incubator of many of the most celebrated doctrines of early Christianity. In fact, we took the students to the ruins of a Roman city that had been packed with churches, complete with baptisteries and parsonages. Even the rubble made it clear that Tunisia had once been a part of a Christian region. In fact, what is now Tunisia once played host to multiple church councils in the third, fourth, and fifth centuries.

Today, there isn't a single indigenous Christian people group left in the nation. There are only a handful of believers, mainly undercover.

I'll never forget the moment I was standing with the students, pointing out an early Christian baptistery in the ruins of a Christian church just as the afternoon call to prayer began at a neighboring mosque. The eerie echo hovered over us as we stood in the ruins of an ancient Christian church. The message was clear. Christianity is dead in Tunisia.

That visit taught me that Christianity can fade away even in the most unlikely places, and it's the responsibility of every generation to preserve the faith and to cover the earth with God's grace.

I also believe that Jesus still performs resurrections, and that one day Tunisia might be a place where God writes one of the most stunning comeback stories in history.

THIS IS OUR MOMENT

Earlier I told you about a widow with five children whom I met in the Dabaab refugee camp where hundreds of thousands of Somali refugees had fled for their lives. It was in that refugee camp that the weight of our responsibility to cover the earth with grace, and the promise of the opportunity before us, hit me between the eyes.

It was within a few feet of where I met that dear widow that two Spanish aid workers were kidnapped by Islamic extremists and carried off into Somalia to face an uncertain fate.

One week after their abduction, I arrived to find the camps unnervingly quiet. I saw only a couple of foreign aid workers—the rest had left because of the threat of further terrorist activity.

The widow with five children told me that she was happy to see my face because she thought the people who were taking care of them had all left because of fear. I didn't have the heart to tell her that I was only passing through, and would, for other reasons, be leaving too.

In a world of a billion Christians, there should never be a moment on the planet when hurting people feel orphaned by God.

Jesus is asking us to join him in the trenches.

AFTERWORD

You can recognize the voice of someone who loves you even in a crowded room. The room can be awash with noise and bustling with people, but if that particular person calls your name, you can hear it. It pierces through the ambient noise and lands in your ear. You perk up, turn your head, and find that person because *he or she is talking directly to you*.

I'm hoping that somehow, the message of this book has cut through the mayhem of the world and landed in that deeply personal way in your heart.

Of course, I know that we have a tendency to read books the way we read the Bible: with *other people* in mind. We think that what we're reading applies to *them* more than to *us*. We say, "Boy, I wish _____ would read this." Sometimes, we even buy them a copy and leave it secretly on their desks with a little anonymous note: "I really thought this would bless you." What we really mean is, "Boy, I hope this book fixes what I don't like about you."

What about what we don't like about *us*?

It's in our human nature to spot the speck in another's eye, and to think that others need more grace than we do.

But, you know I wrote this for you, right?

Every morning, for some time now, I've been in this office chair well before six in the morning. My single cup of espresso sits on my left, the pale yellow lamp above me illuminates this keyboard I'm typing on, and I keep the blinds open so I can slowly watch the sun rise.

I've written this book to *you*, and I have tried to write in such a way that you can almost see me looking into your eyes, almost hear my voice.

I don't know whether I've succeeded. But I've tried to convey that I believe in you, that God loves you, and that there's a world around you that needs a certain kind of grace that only you can give.

I write before my day job. Before the phone starts ringing and the e-mails start dinging and my calendar goes nuts, reminding me of the half dozen people I need to see and the things I need to do. Before all of that chaos, I have been coming into this quiet little place to write to you, feeling a little like Paul when he would write letters to the believers he loved around the world.

I've typed and deleted, edited and rewritten. I've imagined you holding this book as you are now, there in your own chair, in your own special place. Maybe the pages are tattered and dog-eared by this point, or maybe your e-book is filled with highlights and notes. Maybe you've posted a quote or two on Facebook or Twitter.

At least, I hope you have. I hope you've climbed into its pages and applied it to your life.

Authors write on the chance that someone will read what they've written, and that someone will be blessed by it. It's clear that you've read it, if you've made it this far, but I also hope you've been blessed by it. And even more than being blessed, I hope that somehow you've been changed. I hope that people will start noticing that you're a person of grace more now than you once were. That your very presence makes your church, or your town or your workplace, a better place, and that your contribution to the world will be filled with the love and grace of Jesus.

I hope that you'll be *salt* that seasons the earth and *light* that illuminates its dark places. I hope you'll be a source of hope for the hopeless, and that'll you'll spend time with those who need Jesus more than anything else in the world. I hope you'll give your money and time, your heart and your energy, and that you'll take personally your part in Jesus' mission to heal a broken world. I hope you will follow him not just into the palaces we've built and that we call sanctuaries, but into the slums and orphanages as well—that you'll bear the burdens of widows and care for the elderly and make sure that the present suffering of many alive today will not also be a prophecy of their future. I hope that you'll work with me to free this world of the chains of spiritual darkness, suffering, and poverty—of child labor and sexual slavery, of abuse and evil, of hatred, pain, and loneliness.

We all know someone *right now* who needs help to keep going on. I hope, today, we'll each do something about it.

———

You're at the end of this book now.

Once you turn its final page, you will become your own kind of book, hopefully filled with stories of the grace of Jesus.

This moment is not only the *end* of this book. It's also the book's most important moment. This is the moment in which you will decide: Will you simply shelve what you've read? Or will you close the book, look honestly at yourself in the mirror, and decide what could happen in your life if you decided to become, fully, a person of grace?

The world needs you.

Your friend,

@JohnnieM

Facebook.com/JohnnieOnline

ABOUT THE AUTHOR

JOHNNIE MOORE IS AN AUTHOR, ADVISER, pastor, professor, and vice president of Liberty University.

Whether it's helping manage the day-to-day operations of one of the world's largest universities (with more than 92,000 students), teaching world religions on the ground in Israel or in India, or leading North America's largest weekly gathering of Christian college students (10,000+), Johnnie is out to make a difference in his generation.

And he has literally trekked across the globe doing it. His missionary and humanitarian adventures have taken him to more than twenty nations. He has talked with genocide victims in Bosnia and Rwanda, learned Buddhism from the Dalai Lama's personal archivist in the Himalayas, observed Hindu rituals on the banks of the Ganges River, and watched more than two thousand Indian Christians take a martyr's oath before receiving their diplomas. On three different occasions he has visited places that were later bombed by Islamic extremists, and during one of his fourteen trips to India he even witnessed a parade celebrating the piety of a Jain priest who had lived his entire life naked.

His work at Liberty University and abroad has prompted national leaders in education, politics, and religion to consult with Moore on the challenge of translating their message and preparing their organizations for the rise of America's eighty million millennials. He serves on the board of trustees of World Help.

His first book, *Honestly: Really Living What We Say We Believe*, prompted Douglas Gresham to say, "I am convinced that Jack (my stepfather C. S. Lewis) would both enjoy and applaud this book."

Johnnie and his dear wife, Andrea, live in Virginia and spend their free time in sunny places around the world, reading books.

TWITTER: @JOHNNIEM
FACEBOOK: FACEBOOK.COM/JOHNNIEONLINE
www.johnniemoore.org
www.liberty.edu
www.worldhelp.net

ACKNOWLEDGMENTS

To ANDREA—Thank you for going this way with me, being an encouragement over each step, and giving me the joy of calling you my love. Our adventure is just beginning.

To CARA AND SHAWN (AND JOSIAH AND ELIANA) AND JOSH AND CHRISTI—Thank you for doing life with us, and teaching us what real friends look like.

To JERRY AND BECKI—Thanks for being behind us, and granting us the privilege of serving at Liberty during such an important moment in history.

To RON AND CAROL—Thanks for introducing us and being such good godparents. The investment you've made in our lives is incalculable.

To RUBENS AND ELIANA—Thanks for welcoming me into your family, supporting me in every moment of this project, and offering your home as our own.

To FELIPE AND LELA—Thanks for being such a wonderful brother and sister, and thanks for being such an encouragement to us.

To DAD—Thanks for being my biggest fan and my best friend and always being behind me. Without question I wouldn't be writing this if it weren't for you.

To MOM AND DWAYNE—Thanks for your prayers and support and for having the faith to lay the foundation for all of this.

To JULIE AND NICK—Thanks for your prayers and your service to our King. Congratulations on your new marriage and all that the future holds.

To MATT BAUGHER, AND THE ENTIRE NELSON TEAM— Thanks for believing in me from the beginning and exhibiting such patience and hard work in making this a reality.

To DAVID LAMBERT—Thanks for lending your extraordinary gift to make this book come together. Your quiet work is changing the world, literally.

To SEALY YATES—Thanks for so generously investing a lifetime of wisdom in this young leader, and for being a new and constant friend.

To DOUGLAS GRESHAM—Thanks for volunteering so many hours to make me a better writer. You have your stepfather's gift, and his generosity too.

To everyone else who gave advice and read earlier drafts and gave brilliant suggestions and taught me how to write and to speak and to love and to live—You've left me stronger by giving me more grace than I've ever deserved.

NOTES

INTRODUCTION
1. My friend Doug Gresham told me this story in an e-mail on September 10, 2011.

CHAPTER 3: THE GOD WITH DIRTY HANDS
1. Max Lucado, *Just Like Jesus* (Nashville: Thomas Nelson, 2003), 32.

CHAPTER 5: JESUS AND THE REJECTS
1. Matthew 13:55–57.
2. John 1:45–46.

CHAPTER 6: GRACE SLEEPS WITH TRUTH
1. John 1:48.
2. John 1:49.
3. Tim Keller podcast.

CHAPTER 8: CHRISTIANS SHOULD BE HAPPY, FOR GOD'S SAKE
1. C. S. Lewis, letter to Sheldon Vanauken, quoted in Vanauken, *A Severe Mercy* (New York: Harper and Row, 1977), 189.
2. Luke 2:10.
3. Timothy Keller, *King's Cross: The Story of the World in the Life of Jesus* (New York: Penguin, 2011), 14–15.

4. John 15:11, emphasis added.
5. C. S. Lewis, *Weight of Glory* (New York: HarperCollins, 1949), 26.
6. The Greek word for *happiness* is a combination of two words. The first means "good" and the second means "spirit." So a very literal translation might be to have a *good spirit*, but what caused, or produced, this *eudaimonia* was a subject of great controversy and discussion between ancient Greek philosophers.
7. Johnnie Moore, *Honestly: Really Living What We Say We Believe* (Eugene, OR: Harvest House, 2011), 108–12.
8. http://history1900s.about.com/od/medicaladvancesissues/a/nobelhistory.htm.

CHAPTER 9: HOW TO MISS THE GRACE OF GOD

1. Steve Farrar, *Finishing Strong: Going the Distance for Your Family* (Colorado Springs, CO: Multnomah Publishers, 1995), 206.
2. William Barclay, *The Acts of the Apostles* (Louisville, KY: Westminster John Knox, 2003), 152–53.
3. Ibid., 152.

CHAPTER 10: WHAT'S GOOD ABOUT DEATH

1. Dinesh D'Souza, *Life After Death: The Evidence* (Washington, DC: Regnery Publishing, 2009), 5.
2. Ibid., 6.
3. John 5:24, emphasis added.
4. William Hazlitt, *Essayist and Critic* (London and New York: Frederick Warne and Co., 1889), 450.
5. 2 Corinthians 4:8–9.
6. 2 Corinthians 4:14.

CHAPTER 11: WHAT TO DO WHEN TERRORISTS KILL YOUR SPOUSE

1. http://www.asianews.it/index.php?/=endart=9054&theme=8&size=A.

2. C. S. Lewis, *Mere Christianity*, HarperCollins ed. (New York: HarperSanFransico, 2001), 49–50.
3. Timothy Keller, *Counterfeit Gods: The Empty Promises of Money, Sex, and Power, and the Only Hope That Matters* (New York: Penguin, 2009), xviii.
4. Hosea 11:1–3 NIV 1984.
5. Jonah 2:8 NIV 1984.

CHAPTER 12: GLADLY STRANGE

1. Gerald L. Sittser, *Water from a Deep Well: Christian Spirituality from Early Martyrs to Modern Missionaries* (Downers Grove, IL: InterVarsity, 2007), 56–57.
2. Chuck Colson, *The Faith: What Christians Believe, Why They Believe It, and Why It Matters* (Grand Rapids: Zondervan, 2008), 14–15.

CHAPTER 13: GOD MIGHT WANT YOU TO FAIL YOUR TEST

1. Dietrich Bonhoeffer, *The Cost of Discipleship* (New York: Touchstone, 1959), 43–45.
2. Ibid., 45.

CHAPTER 14: CRACKING PANDORA'S BOX

1. James 2:10, paraphrased.
2. Galatians 1:11–13.
3. Acts 9:26.

CHAPTER 15: A GRACE-STARVED PLANET

1. The cost of providing food by World Help at the time of writing this book. See www.worldhelp.net for more information.
2. From the factsheets on the website of the International Justice Mission (www.ijm.org).
3. World Vision, "About Hunger: Hunger Facts," http://www.worldvision.org/content.nsf/learn/hunger-facts?open&lpos=rgt_txt_hunger-facts.
4. Matthew 9:36 NKJV.
5. Matthew 22:39.

5. Matthew 25:35–40.

CHAPTER 16: GRACE IN THE TRENCHES

1. I previously related this story at http://blog.worldhelp
.net/2011/10/a-true-financial-crisis/.
2. Alvin J. Schmidt, *How Christianity Changed the World* (Grand
Rapids: Zondervan, 2004), 19.
3. Max Lucado, *Grace for the Moment* (Nashville: Thomas Nelson,
2007), 271.
4. C. T. Studd, quoted in John Phillips, *Exploring Psalms*, vol. 2
(Grand Rapids: Kregel, 1988), 196.

CHAPTER 17: HOW TO PERFORM MIRACLES

1. 2 Corinthians 5:20 NKJV.

CHAPTER 18: WHAT COULD HAPPEN IF
GRACE COVERED THE EARTH

1. Bob Unruch, "Martyred: 176,000 Christians in 1 Year,"
WorldNetDaily, April 20, 2010, http://www.wnd.com/2010/04
/143493/.
2. Noelle Knox, "Religion Takes a Back Seat in Western Europe,"
USA Today, August 10, 2005, http://www.usatoday.com/news
/world/2005-08-10-europe-religion-cover_x.htm.
3. See Phillip Jenkins, *The Next Christendom: The Coming of Global
Christianity*, 3rd ed. (New York: Oxford University Press, 2011),
xi–xii, 1–3.
4. The Voice of the Martyrs, "Eritrea," http://www.persecution
.net/eritrea.htm.
5. http://philcooke.com/goals-are-dreams-with-deadlines/.
6. Katherine T. Phan, "Rick Warren Believes Church 'Most
Powerful Weapon' to Fight AIDS," *Christian Post*, July 3, 2011,
http://www.christianpost.com/news/rick-warren-explains
-why-church-is-fastest-way-to-fight-aids-51840/.
7. http://thepeaceplan.com/.
8. http://www.thewords.com/articles/mugger5.htm.
9. *Bread and Wine: Readings for Lent and Easter* (Maryknoll, NY:
Orbis Books, 2005), 281–82.